Community Cats

Also by Anne E. Beall, Ph.D.

Strategic Market Research

The Psychology of Gender

Reading the Hidden Communications around You

Community Cats

A journey into the world of feral cats

ANNE E. BEALL, PH.D.

iUniverse

COMMUNITY CATS
A journey into the world of feral cats

iUniverse books may be ordered through booksellers or by contacting:

iUniverse
1663 Liberty Drive
Bloomington, IN 47403
www.iuniverse.com
1-800-Authors (1-800-288-4677)

ISBN: 978-1-4917-4236-5 (sc)
ISBN: 978-1-4917-4235-8 (e)

Library of Congress Control Number: 2014913501

Printed in the United States of America.

iUniverse rev. date: 09/08/2014

For Jenny Schlueter, Liz Houtz, Erica
Roewade, and all the people of Tree House—
in gratitude for the work you do.

Contents

Preface

I have always liked the popular quote "Cats were once worshipped as gods ... and they have never forgotten." Cats evince a pride and comport themselves in a way that commands respect. They bestow their trust and affection on those whom they choose, and they do so within their own time frame. Although they may seem aloof, they have strong connections with one another, with other animals, and with us. But they can be subtle in showing their feelings of affection for human beings, and they can give us the impression that they don't need us.

And yet they need us terribly. One need only look at a cat who has been abandoned by its caretakers to see the impact that such abandonment and neglect can have on a cat. It is an unfortunate reality that many of the stray cats who live outdoors were once house pets. Street life, especially when it's forced on a cat suddenly and unexpectedly, can be a pitiful existence. Cats taken to shelters may not fare much better. More than 1.5 million cats, left at shelters daily, are eventually euthanized each year. They clearly need us. But it turns out that we need them too.

Our partnership with cats began when we transitioned from nomadic hunters into farmers who needed to store grains. Rodents became a problem that cats were able to solve for us (Morris 2011). Although we may think of them as house pets, cats have historically had an important function. But we've forgotten that part of history. How interesting that, in 2013, I would learn about a unique program called Cats at Work in Chicago that uses feral cats to control rodents. After enrolling in the program, I began to tell the neighbors about this unique, new idea. History comes full circle.

When my husband and I first enrolled in Cats at Work, we were concerned about our ability to ensure the safety of the cats we would be hosting and to see that they were well cared for. They had a job to do, and we rejoiced when they did it. But along the way, I became fascinated with them, how they lived, what connections they formed to each other, and how they related to us. They taught me some important lessons. They taught me to be patient and to accept them for who they were, not for what I wanted them to be. If this arrangement was going to work, it would have to work within their parameters—not mine. And I learned that over time they would come to trust us slowly and surely. These working cats, whom I came to know and respect, also taught me about cats in general, and I came to see my indoor cat differently and to understand her better.

I became so enamored of the Cats at Work program that I reached out to other caretakers and to leaders of this movement to learn more about the world of feral cats. My small world of three feral cats widened, and I gathered the stories of caretakers and people who make these programs possible. I learned a lot from every person I interviewed. But what I learned most importantly is that we are all connected and that when we help other creatures, we are rewarded for it in many ways.

I realized that these programs have an enormous impact on the caretakers, on the neighbors around them, and on the cats themselves. It has been a tremendous journey for me, and I wanted to share it with you.

Acknowledgments

Many people have helped me in my quest to understand feral cats and the unique world they inhabit. The first person I am indebted to is Liz Houtz, who became our family's first connection to Tree House. She came over to see if we would be acceptable caretakers and walked us through the entire process. She has been incredibly patient with me and has fielded numerous phone calls and answered a multitude of questions. And she is always up for hearing the latest adventures of my cats, no matter how trivial. This book could not have been written without her help.

I would also like to thank Jenny Schlueter, who sat with me for several hours and explained the history of TNR (Trap-Neuter-Return) and its impact on Chicago. She has been a tremendous resource for facts and figures and has connected me with many of the caretakers I interviewed for this book. Jenny's passion knows no bounds. After visiting a caretaker in her area, I went to her house and saw the amazing setup she has for her feral cat colony. She lives TNR day and night.

Erica Roewade put up with many e-mails and phone calls and took me out one night in the middle of winter to show me what it's like to do her job every day. We trapped cats in frigid temperatures and transported them to the Bucktown clinic to get spayed or neutered. She is extraordinarily patient with the many clients she serves, and she put up with me tagging along and peppering her with questions.

The caretakers whom I spoke to for this book took time out of their schedules, met with me in person, and sent me photos of their cats. They also reviewed their chapters to ensure that I had not represented anything inaccurately. I want to thank Paul, Yvette, Jennie, Katie, Dean, Virginia, and Howard. After visiting with all of you, I learned what a huge difference you make in so many cats' and people's lives.

Dara Salk was very helpful to me and encouraged me to come over and learn how she and her office promote the Cats at Work program in the 47th Ward. She tackles a wide variety of problems, and she took valuable time out of her busy day to chat with me in between fielding calls and requests from her many constituents.

I particularly want to thank Becky Robinson, who spent many hours talking to me about the history of TNR in this country, her own background, and the founding of Alley Cat Allies. She also provided me with research findings about the vacuum effect and how TNR stabilizes and reduces feral cat populations. You have inspired me tremendously.

I also want to thank my colleagues at Beall Research, who helped me write and analyze the survey referenced in this book. I specifically want to thank Sangdi Chen, Michael Taylor, and Tammy Corrigan. I also want to thank Dan Ryan at Decipher, who managed and fielded the study.

Last, I want to thank my husband, Doug, who has been incredibly supportive of this endeavor, despite the fact that it has consumed many of my weekends and evenings. He also takes great care of our indoor cat and our outdoor colony. You are an incredible partner.

Until one has loved an animal, a part of one's soul remains unawakened.
—Anatole France

The greatness of a nation and its moral progress can
be judged by the way its animals are treated.
—Mahatma Gandhi

CHAPTER 1

How It All Began

IT ALL STARTED WHEN A rat ran over my husband's foot. The city of Chicago had just fixed our sidewalk, and we surmised that the construction had disturbed the rats' homes and that they were trying to relocate. We saw rats at all times of the day and night. The rat on my husband's foot (right in front of our home) was the last straw. We mentioned the incident to a neighbor, Tim Cole, who told us about a program called Cats at Work where we could get feral cats who would take care of the rat problem.

We had experienced rat problems for a long time. We live off an alley behind several restaurants, so it's a natural place for rats to live. Rats are part of urban life. And all city dwellers get used to seeing them every so often. However, we became concerned because they were around our home and under our garage. And they seemed to be proliferating. A neighbor told us that if rats build enough tunnels under a structure, it can collapse. So we tried a variety of methods to get rid of them. Nothing really worked. So there I was, looking up this program on the Internet, wondering if a feral cat colony would work for us.

ANNE E. BEALL, PH.D.

TREE HOUSE

We learned that Tree House had a Cats at Work program, and we applied to become one of the program's managed colony caretakers. We were accepted after showing that we could make a commitment to the cats, and we were soon in touch with Liz Houtz, the Community Cats program manager at Tree House. We applied to have a colony of three cats. Liz told us that we needed to feed them twice a day and provide them with a litter box and that Tree House would supply us with outdoor shelters, an outdoor cat box, and a heated water/feeding bowl for our cold Chicago winters.

Our cats were scheduled to arrive on a Sunday. Liz arrived with the makings for a large cage (about eight by four feet), two outdoor shelters, a litter box, and another box that could be used for feeding. And Liz's colleague arrived with three tabby cats in three small cages. She put them on the steps, and immediately one of the cages started rocking. That cat wanted to get out!

My husband, Liz, and I set up the large cage and put the shelters into the cage along with the litter box. We live in a hundred-year-old graystone building in Lakeview, and we put the cage underneath our front stairs and porch. It's actually a large enclosure that is outside of the rain and cold, and Liz felt it would be a great place for the cats to acclimate. She explained that they needed to be in the cage for the first three weeks while they got used to the environment and the sounds around them. They also needed to get used to a new feeding schedule and new caretakers.

After we set up the large cage for them, we opened up the little cat cages, and they ran quickly into the large cage and right into their shelters. We barely saw them. We closed the cage and let them get used to their new surroundings.

Our cat colony arrived in early November, before it got really cold in Chicago. We were one of the last people to get a cat colony for that year, so we felt lucky. And so it began.

2

CHAPTER 2

First Weeks

I FELT SOME TREPIDATION ABOUT taking care of three feral cats. I've had cats my whole life, but house cats and feral cats are not the same. It was obvious to me from the beginning that these cats were not used to humans and that they were afraid of us. Every time I would get near the cage, they would run to the back of it or run into their shelters.

We fed them in the morning and in the evening, and every time I opened the cage I felt a little nervous. I just wasn't sure what to expect, and I wanted to look after them. I also felt that they could provide a great service to us. But I didn't want them to run away, get hit by a car, or get hurt in any way as a result of coming to live in our neighborhood.

INTRODUCTION TO TNR

Our cats were part of the TNR (trap-neuter-return) program; cat advocates practicing TNR *trap* free-roaming cats, have them *neutered* (or spayed) and medically treated, and *return* them to the area where they were living (or relocate them if the area is deemed unsafe). So, they were already fixed. I learned from Liz that they came from the Cragin neighborhood in Chicago and that they had been part of a large colony that had gotten too big. Apparently neighbors were complaining about the cats. The Tree House Community Cats folks had gone over there with humane traps and had put food into them. When the cat goes into the humane trap, the back closes, and then it can be transported. I figured that we probably got the hungriest ones because they ran into the traps first.

Liz said that the cats had a microchip implanted in them (as most pets do) so that, if they got lost, they could be scanned and any vet could identify that they were registered to us. Our name, address, and telephone number were stored on the microchip. My indoor cat, Sarina, has a microchip for the same reason. I was glad to learn that the TNR program was taking this step. I also learned that our colony was registered with the city of Chicago through Tree House.

THREE TABBY CATS WITH DIFFERENT PERSONALITIES

The three cats were of different sizes. One of them was a small male tabby with short hair whom we named Duke. And the other two were female tabby cats with long hair, who looked very similar. We named them Allie and Eloise. One was a little reddish in color with some black on her tail—that was Eloise. The other was Allie, who was less red and had more black on her tail. But even after several months, I still had difficulty telling them apart.

Within the first week, whenever I went down to feed the cats, Duke would come right over and eat in front of us. He seemed to be the least shy. At first I was worried that he wanted to get out of the cage, but he just wanted to eat. And he had no qualms about getting somewhat near to us when the bowl was put out. Allie and Eloise never came near us when we put food out for them. We would have to leave the area in order for them to come out and eat.

Both Allie and Eloise were missing a part of the tip of their left ear. I learned that that is one of the indications that a feral cat has been neutered so it's not trapped again unnecessarily. However, Duke was not missing a tip of his ear, and so I asked Liz about it. She said that someone had tried to socialize him so he could be adopted as a house pet. Apparently these attempts had been unsuccessful, so he'd stayed in the feral cat colony. Liz said that the vet could correct the oversight when Duke was brought in for his annual checkup but that clipping his ear was not necessary at this stage.

We cleaned their litter box every day, tried to keep the cage as clean as possible, and waited for the three weeks to elapse so we could move into the next phase of colony caretaking. We called Liz before the date and asked her what we needed to do, and she told us to wait until the evening to open the cage. She said we could put some of their urine waste around the yard so that they smelled something familiar and added that it's not unusual for members of the colony or for the entire colony to take off for a period of time—sometimes as long as several days or weeks. She told us not to worry if that happened.

Finally, after three weeks, it was time to let them out of the cage. We fed them at the usual time and then opened the cage and waited to see what would happen.

CHAPTER 3

Freedom

IT WAS ACTUALLY THE WEEKEND after Thanksgiving in 2013 when we opened the cage and let Allie, Eloise, and Duke out into our neighborhood for the first time. My son was home from college, and he, my husband, and I went out and stood on the steps above their enclosure to see their reaction after we opened their cage.

Duke was the first one out. He bounded up the stairs from his enclosure and went into our front yard and then across the sidewalk onto the parkway of our home where we had been having problems with rats. He went right to the rat hole and started sniffing it. Then he wandered underneath the cars parked on the street in front of our house and then into the next-door neighbor's yard. We watched him with tremendous nervousness and excitement. Where would he go? Would he wander back to the cage? Would he take off for a while as Liz had suggested? We watched him run around the neighbor's yard and then run right back into the enclosure and back into the cage.

Allie and Eloise were more hesitant and climbed to the top of the steps and then back down to the cage when they heard a noise or when someone walked by. They finally emerged onto the sidewalk and then into the neighbor's yard but, within a few minutes, rushed back to their home under our stairs. And Duke was back and forth too. I could have watched them all night. I was so worried they would run into the street or run into the alley and get hurt, but they seemed to venture out for brief periods and then run back to the cage.

FIRST DAYS OF FREEDOM AND A DISAPPEARANCE

When I went to feed the trio on the subsequent days, they were always in the cage waiting for their wet and dry food. We never left food in the cage overnight or during the day because Liz said it would attract other wildlife. So at the usual time of day, the three cats were always present. I was starting to feel that everything was going pretty well and that I didn't need to worry. And then Eloise disappeared.

It occurred a few days later when I went to feed them at the regular time, and only two cats were in the cage. I wondered if perhaps Eloise was just hiding or if she was too nervous to come out. She never came close to me at feeding time as Duke did, but I would always see her nevertheless. But this time I didn't see her. And when I picked up the food bowls, it was clear that only two cats had eaten. I didn't see her for several days, and I suspected that something terrible had happened to her. I was pretty upset. I felt responsible for these creatures, and I felt that I had already failed.

A few days later, Eloise reappeared at mealtime and seemed to be her usual self. She didn't look as though she was in poor health or as if anything bad had happened. She actually seemed like she was happy to be back with Allie and Duke. I was ecstatic.

After another couple of weeks, we dismantled the cage, swept out the entire enclosure, and put an old memory foam bathmat we were no longer using on top of one of the shelters and then covered the top of that with an old towel so the cats would have a soft place to sit. And we moved a table into the enclosure so that I could see them eating through the downstairs window and see if everyone was eating at mealtime. I would set their food up on the table and then go back inside to watch. Everything seemed like it was going well.

CHAPTER 4

Rats!

THE CATS DEFINITELY WERE HANGING around the places where we had seen rats. My husband had seen one of the females, Allie or Eloise, out prowling around our garage where we had a massive rat problem. Liz had told us that just the presence of the cats would encourage the rats to leave, even if the cats didn't hunt them. I figured that, even if the cats discouraged the rats from living around us, that that would be good enough. I had a hard time believing that my three new furry friends would actually kill any rats.

A couple of weeks after the cats had been out of their cage, a neighbor sent us a text that he had seen Duke kill a rat right on his patio. I was incredulous. I asked him how he knew it was one of our cats and whether he had seen the deed occur. He gave us a perfect description of Duke stalking the rat and attacking it with vehemence.

A few days later, I came down to pick up the food dishes, and there was a large, dead rat right at the bottom of the steps going into their enclosure. I was so excited that I ran back up into the house yelling to my husband. "Come look! Come look! They've killed a rat!" The next day, we found another one.

One morning, I went out to feed them, and Eloise was perched on the front step and was looking very intently at something along the side of our house. I couldn't see a thing. I had her food, but she wasn't interested at all. She ran down the steps and along the side of the house and grabbed something in her mouth. Allie appeared close behind her, and when they went into the light I could see that what they had captured was a rat. That happened on several occasions. Eloise was an incredible hunter.

HARDWORKING CATS

Clearly the program was working, and we were thrilled. After so many years of fighting the rats, we were starting to win. In addition to seeing the dead rats, we noticed many fewer rats in the neighborhood. Several neighbors also told us that they were seeing fewer rats.

We also noticed that many of the rat holes disappeared over time. Liz told us that putting some of the cat urine waste into the holes would be a strong deterrent for the rats. So that's what we did. We kept checking on these holes, and they were not reopening, which meant that either the rats were finding somewhere else to enter and exit or they had moved along (or been sent to rat heaven—by our cats). We began to affectionately refer to our cat colony as *the Rat Pack*, and we wrote a testimonial to Tree House about how effective their program had been for us.

Everything was going according to plan when the polar vortex hit and sent Chicago temperatures to -15 degrees Fahrenheit. Winter had hit Chicago, and it was brutal.

CHAPTER 5

Christmas and the Polar Vortex

THAT CHRISTMAS, WE WENT AWAY on our family vacation, and we had our cat sitter at the time, Kari, look after Sarina and our colony outside. I was a bit nervous about leaving them, but one has to let go. Kari also took care of a cat colony near her home, so we knew she would do a good job.

When we got back from our trip, I immediately went to see how the colony was doing. Kari had rearranged their quarters and had left a note telling me that she had moved their shelters so they would be out of view of people walking by and that she had opened a window to the lower porch area outside our home so the cats had a point of entry and egress. She explained that humans might cause the most harm to the cats and that she was just trying to protect them.

Then she told me about "Trapper John," aka John Norton, who lives in Chicago and drives around in a truck trapping feral cats. I immediately went online to learn about this person and found a couple of articles about him, along with a warning from other feral cat colony caretakers.

Trapper John was fired from animal control and had a long history of trapping feral cats. The people at Tree House told me that whole colonies had disappeared as a result of him. He claimed that he was trapping the cats because of his belief that allowing cats to live outside is inhumane and that euthanizing them was a better option. He didn't care if he was taking cats that were in a registered colony or not. I took note of how he looked, got a description of the truck, and sent a photo of him around to the neighbors, asking that they call the police if they saw him in the area. Suddenly I became afraid for my cats' lives.

I began to think about whether Trapper John's viewpoint might be right. Was it better for the cats to be euthanized than to live under our porch and get fed twice a day and run around our yard? I would be seriously tested on this question when we learned that a polar vortex was coming and that it would bring some of the coldest days to Chicago.

THE POLAR VORTEX ARRIVES

I had lived in Chicago for sixteen years, and I had never experienced a winter that was this cold. It was -15 degrees Fahrenheit with wind chills of 30 degrees below. When the cold arrived, I closed up the window that was blowing cold air into the area and put a towel and sheet over the window to provide a little insulation. I put blankets on top of the cats' shelters and made sure that their houses were out of the wind. I changed their water in the morning and night because it would freeze during the day, and I fed them twice a day as usual. And I watched them closely to see how they were doing. At any sign of distress, I was ready to call Tree House.

Over the course of those cold days, the cats came out of their shelters when I came down with food, and they ate all of it. My son, Michael, said that eating a lot of food was probably keeping them warm. Immediately after they ate, they went right back into their shelters. They stayed put for those few days but ate a lot, used the litter box, and generally seemed fine. As soon as it warmed up to 15 degrees Fahrenheit, they were out and about as usual. They even seemed happy to be frolicking in the yard. They suffered no ill effects from the extreme weather, and I knew at that point that a life outside was certainly better than no life at all. I was still worried about Trapper John, but I knew I was doing the right thing.

CHAPTER 6

Eloise

THE THREE CATS HAD VERY different personalities, but they each blossomed in unique ways. Duke, who was the youngest and smallest, was the only boy, and he rushed toward the food every time we brought it into the cats' enclosure. Over the first few months, Duke became less bold, and Eloise became the one who approached us first when we brought food to the Rat Pack. Allie continued to remain aloof during those initial months. At first, she would never eat in my presence. She would scamper out the window when I placed food on their feeding table. But over time, she became less afraid of me and would eat when I was in their area. But she would not let me get close to her.

I fed them in the morning and early evening, and I would always announce that I was coming down to them with a singsong hello as I opened my front door. Then I would walk down to the front steps and down another set of stairs to their living area. As soon as Eloise heard the door and the sound of my voice, she would run up from her area up to the top of the stairs to my front door. I would get the "royal escort" down to the bottom of our stairs and then down to her area. She would walk just a few steps ahead of me. And when I put her food on the table, she would jump right up and eat in front of me. She wasn't the least bit afraid. In comparison, the other cats would wait until I had walked away from the table to eat.

UNEXPECTED, SWEET INTERACTIONS

One evening after feeding the cats, I picked up the empty cat bowls and walked up the stairs to my front door. I noticed Eloise following me, so I decided to sit on my front steps with her for a while and admire her lovely brown-reddish coat. I sat on the top step and just talked to her very gently. And I was careful not to look her in the eye too much because I had learned that behavior is threatening to cats. So I talked to her and blinked at her with long blinks. And then something amazing happened. She came over to me and rubbed up against me. I reached down and petted her on the head, and she rubbed against me again. I was completely taken aback. A feral cat rubbing up against a person and wanting to be petted? Was this possible?

I decided to do some research, and I learned that feral cats sometimes let their caretakers pet them because they view them as surrogate parents (almost like a mother) and that they bond to a specific caretaker. However, the article I read also warned that that does not mean that the feral cat can be socialized to live with humans. They simply aren't used to being in a household and would find it very difficult. And they cannot transfer their affections onto another human—just the caretaker. I wasn't sure what to believe. I talked to Kari, and she said that caretakers are divided about petting. Some caretakers believe that feral cats should not be petted and that the cats should be somewhat afraid of humans, given what some people may do to them. Others believe it's okay. I decided that I would let the cats let me know what they needed.

And so Eloise and I had many sweet interactions. Sometimes, she would let me pet her and she would seek me out to rub against me. At other times, she was very shy and avoided any type of contact. It was sometimes hard to tell what mood she was in, but I let her be my guide. At times, she would wait outside the front door after a feeding and look for me. On several occasions, I'd look at her through a window and she'd meow at me. I could never resist that. I would go out, and we would have a petting session on my porch. She would come to me and then rub against my hand, and then I would pet her. She would often get very close to me and then circle behind my back and then come next to me and let me pet her again.

SIDEWALK AND STAIRWAY GREETINGS

One morning, I came out of the house to pick up the food dishes. I saw Eloise on the sidewalk in front of a neighbor's house. When she saw me, she ran down the sidewalk and jumped through our fence and ran up to me as if to greet me. She let me pet her a few times and then went on her way. It wasn't feeding time, and there was nothing other than affection that she wanted at that time. She and I were creating a close bond.

A couple of times during those first few months, we went on vacation and we would be away for a couple of days. We would have someone take care of the cats and feed them at the regular times. Whenever I would return, I would announce myself at the top of my steps, and Eloise would come running up—faster than usual. It was almost as if she missed me. I certainly missed her, and I would pet her for several minutes. I would put their food down in their area and then walk back up the stairs to my front door. Eloise wouldn't touch the food and would come upstairs and sit at the top of the step where I would pet her again. Then she would go back down and eat her food.

One day when I went to pick up the empty food dishes, Eloise followed me up to the outer front door and meowed as if she was asking to come in. I opened the outer door that leads to the hallway in front of our entry door, and she slipped into the hallway. She purred very loudly as she nuzzled against me.

Eloise

CHAPTER 7

The Neighbors

WHEN WE FIRST GOT THE cats, I talked to all of the neighbors in our area and asked them if they had any issues with our taking care of a colony. I wanted to make sure we didn't have trouble down the road with people complaining that we had not informed them before making this decision. Everyone whom we talked to was keen on the idea. Though some weren't sure if the cats would really solve the rat problem, no one objected to the plan.

When we first began, I was amazed how many people would walk by and ask how the cats were doing. During the time period when we first let them out of the cage and Eloise disappeared, people would ask if she had come back. They were concerned for their new four-legged neighbors. Almost every time I was outside that first winter, people would ask how the cats were doing with the inclement weather and whether they were okay. It was quite touching. And often people would walk by with their dogs and mention that they often saw their new "friends," the cats.

One day when I was outside cleaning the cats' litter box, a woman I hardly knew came over to me and asked about the cats. I told her they were doing well, and she told me that she was so pleased that the cats were taking care of the rats because she didn't want the city of Chicago to put rat poison in her yard. She'd had an interaction with a city worker during which she'd instructed him not to put rat poison in her yard because she had young children. He'd argued with her, but she'd remained adamant. "We don't need it. We have the Cats at Work program here," she'd told him proudly.

The neighbors were particularly important because it turns out our cats were wandering a fair bit around the neighborhood. One neighbor told us that our cats liked to go down and watch the birds at the bird feeder toward the end of the block. He told us that he regularly saw them there every morning. They never caught a bird, but they certainly liked to watch them.

WHERE DO THEY GO?

I became interested in exactly where the Rat Pack was going. One day when it snowed, I saw a set of paw prints and I decided to follow them. The prints showed that one of the cats had gone out the front of our house, onto the sidewalk, and then down the pathway of the house next door. I followed the paw prints and they went behind the neighbors' house and down into their open basement area into a room filled with garden furniture and garden tools. I went down into the area and turned on a light. And there was Allie. She was sitting comfortably on a pile of seat cushions that were on top of a shelf. It was a tall pile of cushions that was probably very soft. As soon as she saw me, she went to another area where I couldn't see her. I had found one of their hideouts. So I let her be. However, I told one of the neighbors who lived in the house that my cats were hanging out in their open basement alcove. He said he didn't mind, and I was so thankful.

Another neighbor, Paul Lisnek, was especially kind and offered to help us financially with the cats. He made that offer numerous times. I always told him that it wasn't necessary, but finally one day I relented. He asked us if he could do something for them, and I said he could buy them a couple of cans of cat food. That afternoon, I came home and found a case of cat food on the porch with a note from him. I was stunned. He gave me food many times, and I was always grateful. It turned out that feeding them cost us about two dollars per day, which added up. However, the cost was definitely worth the rewards.

On another occasion, I received a text from Paul asking if the cats were okay. He had been told by a tenant that there was a dead animal near his garage, and he was worried that maybe something had happened to one of our cats. I happily replied that all our cats were fine and that it was most likely a dead rodent!

One night, we had a big storm with a great deal of rain, and several neighbors were out late at night putting sand bags around their homes and garages to keep them from flooding. Apparently, the alley around our home had completely filled with water. I later learned that several neighbors came down in the middle of the night to check on the cats and see if they were okay. It was very touching to see how many people cared about the Rat Pack.

CHAPTER 8

Sarina

AS OF THIS WRITING, SARINA has been with us for thirteen years. I adopted her from Anti-Cruelty Society in Chicago when she was a kitten, and she's been a sweet addition to our home. She has a strong personality and doesn't care for other cats. At one point, we learned this lesson the hard way when we brought another cat named Samantha home. I'm quite sure we didn't handle the introduction in the right way because it was pretty much a disaster from the beginning. Unfortunately, Samantha had a heart condition that was terminal. She lived with us for a couple of years and then passed away when her heart gave out.

I wasn't all that concerned about how Sarina would feel about having cats living right outside of our house. In the beginning, when I was opening cans of cat food and taking them outside the house, Sarina would meow and follow me to the door. If I had to put a description to her behavior I would say she was perplexed. I'm sure she was wondering why I was taking such lovely treats outside the home when she was clearly right there. When I came back into the house, she would always be waiting for me.

INTEREST ON BOTH SIDES OF THE GLASS

I assumed that indoor and outdoor cats lived in different spheres and never the twain shall meet. I wasn't correct. One day, Eloise was in front of our house looking into our window and Sarina was looking back very intently on the other side of the glass. They both stared at each other, but neither made a sound.

Sarina was always somewhat interested in the outdoor cats. I would often come into a room and find her at the window that overlooked the side of our house and the walkway next to our neighbor's home. This walkway was used frequently by all of the cats. On several occasions, I saw Eloise, Allie, or Duke looking back at her. They were never hostile toward one another. They just seemed intrigued. And on occasion, Sarina would run from one window to another to see one of the cats moving outside our home.

Sarina

I realized from this experience that I didn't know as much about cats as I'd thought. I started reading about cats and realized that I had a lot to learn about these creatures. I decided that it would be helpful to talk with the folks at Tree House and to meet with other colony caretakers. So I asked Liz if I could talk to another caretaker, and she suggested I chat with Paul. Liz said he had an amazing setup in his garage. I was intrigued.

CHAPTER 9

The Garage Kitties

I WENT OVER TO SEE Paul and his colony on a blustery winter day in early 2014. Paul lives in a small home on a dead-end street in Chicago near the river. The street is very quiet and filled with small frame homes. Paul is a large man, with a full head of black hair, who radiates kindness when you meet him. He was interested in telling me all about his colony, "the Garage Kitties," and how he ended up becoming a caretaker.

Apparently the rat problem in his neighborhood had become unbearable. He saw rats in his backyard all the time, so he put mesh around the underside of his wooden fence to keep them out. Then he tried poison. Nothing worked. He had heard of Cats at Work but was concerned about participating in the program because he thought the neighbors might object. One night as he was sitting out in his backyard, he saw rats running around and wondered what he was going to do. He looked over to the left of his foot and saw a large rat sitting right next to him. He realized that the rat had absolutely no fear of him. It was time to call Tree House.

Tree House brought over three female cats, and he installed them in his garage. After the waiting period, he let them out of their cage and into the garage so they could become accustomed to that space. Within a couple of days, he found four dead rats on the floor and one of the cats, standing over her kills, looking pretty smug. They had gotten four rodents who had been living right in his garage! It was then that the cat got her name, Kevorkian—angel of death. The other two were named Morticia and Eberkineses. These were names that Paul and his friends came up with when they were out canoeing one night.

FIRST DAYS IN THE NEIGHBORHOOD

When the cats were finally let out into the neighborhood, they went on a major rodent cleanup mission. Paul was finding at least two dead rats a week. And these were the ones they were bringing back to the garage—not the ones they were killing and leaving. In the year since he has had them, he has seen over a hundred dead rats. Now he can sit in his backyard in peace. He never sees a live rat anymore.

About two weeks after Paul let the cats out into the neighborhood, they disappeared. The Garage Kitties left around the time he decided to clean his garage, which scared them. They would come back to feed, but they wouldn't stay in the garage. At a neighborhood meeting, Paul sat next to a man who lived across the street, and he asked the man if he was having any rat problems. The neighbor replied, "Not anymore. I just had three cats move into my garage!"

Paul explained that the cats were from his colony, and he redoubled his efforts to make his own garage as cat-friendly as possible.

When I stepped into the garage, I saw that Paul had definitely achieved his objective. He had built structures where the Garage Kitties could climb up and sit on perches; he had several sleeping boxes and a structure in the middle that looked like a yurt—a conical dwelling that he heats when it gets very cold outside. He put a compost bin on top of the yurt, which provided natural heat. I saw two of the cats, who were skittish but well-fed and healthy. They had plenty of places to sit and hide. And Paul had put a small cat flap on one of the walls of his garage so they could come in and out of the garage at any time. It was a feral cat heaven.

The cats eventually moved back to Paul's garage and have been living there ever since. Paul says they occasionally hang out in the neighbor's garage, which he calls their "Southampton summer residence," but they mostly stay on his property. Morticia is so happy in her garage home that she doesn't leave it much during the winter and heads out only when it gets a bit warmer. Paul beamed when he said, "They have a great life here."

"Where did the cats come from?" I asked.

"They came from the Austin neighborhood, where a woman had been feeding about twenty cats who hadn't been fixed. Tree House came in and trapped the group and had them spayed and neutered. But it turns out there weren't twenty cats at all; there were forty! The woman didn't even know how many cats she had been feeding."

"What did they do with all the cats?"

"Because the colony was so large, they relocated some of the cats to other areas of the city."

"Are there a lot of people feeding cats like that?" I asked.

"I don't know," he said slowly, "but if you feed cats that haven't been fixed, you can have a real problem on your hands."

"Really?" I was surprised by his seriousness.

"You may start feeding a couple of cats, and before you know it, they have kittens; and then three cats become twenty," he explained. "I wouldn't feed any strays without getting them neutered. It doesn't take long for the population to get out of hand."

After a moment, I decided to switch the subject. "I know your cats are killing a lot of rats. But what about birds—are your cats killing them at all?" I asked.

His reply came quickly. "I've only found evidence that they've killed two birds. I think the rats are what they like to hunt, and the rats are keeping them pretty busy given that we live near the river, which is where we have a lot of rats."

FOSTERING FERAL CATS

After going to the garage, Paul and I entered his home, and he showed me three cats he's fostering right now. I asked him what "fostering cats" meant, and he said it involves socializing them and caring for them until they can be adopted. The foster cats were three orange tabby cats named Roscoe, Addison, and Belmont. They were feral cats who had been trapped, neutered, and returned to their area. But their colony caretaker thought they could be socialized to become indoor housecats. All of the cats were eleven months old, which meant that they had missed a critical window of time (in other words, the first few months of life) when they can be socialized. However, the caretaker of the colony said that the cats were so friendly that it might be possible for them to make that transition.

Addison was sitting near Paul's chair in the dining room, and he was the friendliest of the group. Paul had been fostering him, and then he was put up for adoption at a local shelter. There, he was put into a cage while the shelter found someone to adopt him. Addison had never been in a cage before, and it overwhelmed him. He stopped eating and hissed at people who came near him. Paul stepped in to take him back home. Addison had made great progress and was just about ready to be adopted when I took a photo of Paul holding him. He was going back to Tree House, which doesn't use cages, so he could be put up for adoption.

Before I left, I asked, "What have you learned from the experience of having the feral cats both indoors and outdoors?"

He thought for a moment and replied, "Cats are very resilient. They live in all kinds of situations, and they manage to thrive. It's amazing. Even when it was very cold out, they did okay. But they also need us. They really need us to help them. I can see that with the feral cats who are indoors. I spend a fair amount of time with them, but when I don't work them every day, they take a step back."

As I started to leave, I began to think that the relationship between caregivers and cats was fairly symbiotic. They help us and we help them.

My next stop was Tree House to learn more about the program and to see if I could talk with other caretakers.

Addison

CHAPTER 10

A Visit to Tree House and How TNR Came to Chicago

I ARRIVED AT TREE HOUSE in early February 2014. I'd been to animal shelters before but never a place like this one. Tree House is a no-kill, cageless shelter for cats. Their mission is to bring in sick, injured, abused, and neglected stray cats from around the city of Chicago and find homes for them. At the time this book was written, they occupied an old wooden frame house and were building a new state-of-the-art facility in the western part of the city. The house had been a residence at one time and was converted into a shelter in 1975. There were small rooms on every floor, and the place was teeming with cats. On each level, there were cats freely walking around their areas. There were a few cages for the new cats who were making the transition, but it was a place where you could walk into a room and freely approach the cats—and they could freely approach you. Cats could be seen in administrators' offices and in almost every room.

I met with Jenny Schlueter, who is a lovely woman with long, wavy dark chestnut hair and a soft voice. She has a quiet intensity when she speaks. She has an interesting mix of passion and patience, and I could see how these qualities had served her well in her work. She is Tree House's full-time director of development, which is her "day job"; she jokes that her full-time volunteer job is "professional cat lady." As the founder and director of the Community Cats Program at Tree House, she helped bring TNR to Chicago in its current form. She had lived in Spain after college and had practiced TNR at that time when she ran a small cat rescue group there. In Spain, she learned how well cats could do outdoors under the right conditions and how they were accepted as part of the urban landscape. When she came to Tree House ten years ago, there was no formal TNR program in Chicago. A small community of people was doing TNR independently, but the group's efforts weren't coordinated. Jenny wanted to get a feel for the Chicago community first, so she just observed how Tree House worked during the first year. But she did TNR on her own when she came across a colony of cats in her neighborhood.

EARLY YEARS FOR JENNY AT TREE HOUSE

Back in 2004, Tree House accepted all cats based on the urgency of their medical needs, and they didn't differentiate between feral and nonferal cats. Jenny calls feral cats "free-roaming" and divides these cats into "feral," "semiferal," and "friendlies." She noticed that a substantial number of feral cats were living at Tree House at that time, and she became concerned about how long it would take to socialize them in order for them to be adoptable. Although Tree House ran a great socialization program and many cats benefited from it, many others were scared living indoors and they hid from adopters, which made their chances of finding a home almost impossible.

Her other concern was the number of requests Tree House was receiving, which they couldn't meet because they had so many long-term feral residents. Jenny believes that all feral cats can eventually be socialized to be indoor pets, but that it can take several months or years. And the quality of a feral cat's life in a shelter is questionable at best because of the high stress of living indoors. Jenny quickly realized that, if the entire shelter became predominantly filled with feral cats, Tree House would be turning away friendly cats who could be quickly adopted. And that would make it difficult to meet the needs of thousands of stray cats who needed help in Chicago. She also became concerned about the number of calls that Tree House was receiving for feral cats that the organization couldn't address in a timely way.

She decided to help the people who were calling about feral cats with TNR work and spent many hours doing phone counseling as well as humane trapping. She would go out after work and on her days off to trap colonies, have them neutered, and then return them (or relocate them if their lives had been threatened). Jenny often paid for some or all of the spay or neuter surgeries when the person could not afford it. She invested hundreds of dollars of her own money. If the cats were friendly, she taught people how to foster them, and she would get them onto the waiting list at Tree House. Jenny also fostered many cats on her own.

TIME FOR A COORDINATED TNR PROGRAM

As time progressed, Jenny began to see the opportunity for a large-scale program in Chicago, and she began to educate different groups, including her colleagues at Tree House, about the potential for a TNR program. When Tree House executive director Dave de Funiak started to see how effective her after-hours work was, he began to take notice. He was initially intrigued and eventually supportive. He finally agreed to allow Jenny to present her program to the staff and board. Eventually the admission policies were changed, and Tree House mixed feral and semiferal cats with the friendly cats in an effort to get the feral cats socialized more quickly. As more feral cats became socialized and adopted, more spaces opened up to accept friendly cats. Before the end of 2005, the Tree House Feral Friends TNR program (later changed to Community Cats Program) was formalized. In less than a decade, the average number of intakes and adoptions at Trio House more than tripled, partly because of the Community Cats/TNR program. The program has an e-mail and phone counseling line, trapping assistance, a trap bank, a pet food pantry, and monthly TNR workshops, as well as low-cost spay or neuter packages for feral cats. The program is run completely by volunteers.

But the work didn't stop there. Jenny's input was instrumental in bringing about the 2007 ordinance in Chicago (07-O-72) that legalizes the caretaking of feral cat colonies if they are registered with a sponsoring organization. The ordinance clearly spells out that sponsoring organizations like Tree House must manage these colonies, educate caretakers, maintain records, and report annually on the number and location of all colonies, as well as report any caretakers who don't comply with the caretaker requirements. The ordinance lays out what caretakers must do, which includes keeping records, providing appropriate shelters and food and water, and ensuring that the cats get regular vaccinations and veterinary care. Caretakers must also spay or neuter any colony cats and remove any kittens after they have been weaned so they can be adopted. Now in 2014, ten years after she began this program, Jenny beamed when she told me that there are currently 1,055 managed cat colonies with 7,040 cats in Cook County, and Tree House manages 460 of these colonies (2,983 cats).

MAJOR CHALLENGES

Despites all this progress, Jenny admits it's still an uphill battle. Tree House does workshops for different groups in the city, but not all of the animal organizations in Chicago believe in TNR. And very few residents really understand the concept. I certainly didn't understand anything about this program until I read about it online and talked to Jenny and the other folks at Tree House. The opportunity for educating the public is enormous and overwhelming. One of the major issues is a misconception about what constitutes a healthy life for a cat. Over time, Americans have increasingly come to believe that an indoor life is the safest and healthiest life for a cat. Jenny believes that cats who can live indoors should do so with some supervised outdoor enrichment, such as a "catio" (a screened-in area that allows cats to experience the outside) or a backyard secured with a "cat fence" when possible. But feral cats are another matter. They cannot be brought indoors to live if they have not been socialized extensively. And some can never come indoors. Another issue is the term *feral*, which sounds wild and dangerous to people. Some people mistakenly believe that that these cats should all be euthanized—a thought I found absolutely horrific given my own experience.

Other challenges include the cost of feeding cats. Many of the colony caretakers in Chicago are low-income individuals who cannot afford cat food. In response to this problem, Jenny proposed including colony caretakers in the Tree House pet food pantry client list, which provides food to some caretakers. She estimated that the pantry costs Tree House between $15,000 and $20,000 a year, and they cannot even begin to meet the needs of caretakers.

SUCCESS

But despite these challenges, the program appears to be working. When I asked about the impact of TNR on Chicago, Jenny shared the statistics that were presented to Cook County in 2013 by some of the sponsoring organizations—PAWS Chicago, Triple R Pets, and Tree House. (The Anti-Cruelty Society of Illinois also provides low-cost spay and neuter to feral cats but is not a sponsor of the ordinance.) Since 2008, over 17,538 feral cats have been spayed or neutered in Cook County. More than 50 percent of these cats are females, who generally have about two litters a year with an average of three to five cats per litter. A simple calculation is that the program has prevented over 250,000 kittens from being born over the past five years. And considering that many of those kittens would eventually have had kittens of their own, it's not surprising that an analysis of twenty-three zip codes where there were managed colonies showed that the number of colony cats was reduced by 41 percent. As a result, the number of stray and feral cats brought to animal control in those areas has been greatly reduced.

What's even more amazing is that these programs are run at no cost to the city. An article published in the *Chicago Tribune* in 2013 (Doyle 2013) reported that capturing and euthanizing feral cats by the city costs about $245 a cat, which adds up to hundreds of thousands of dollars a year. The sponsoring organizations of the ordinance offer spaying or neutering, vaccinations (including rabies), parasite treatment, microchipping, humane trapping, rehoming of cats who are friendly, and food for colony caretakers who cannot afford it. These services are *funded completely by the private community.*

THE FUTURE

I asked Jenny about her vision for the future, and she said that she would love to have a colony caretaker on every block. Even though that hasn't happened, the program has grown tremendously, and it expands every month as people learn about it. She said that people discover the benefits of TNR and the incredible bonds that they can have with community cats.

These days, Jenny has been focused on the "big picture" issues for the program. She's procuring grants, directing the strategic vision, researching best practices, training and mentoring staff, and promoting the TNR program throughout Chicago. But you can tell that she is most proud of the fact that she has personally done TNR with over 150 cats in her neighborhood since she moved to Humboldt Park. She has also helped thousands of others through hands-on assistance, counseling, workshops, and seminars.

"What is the most rewarding part of your job?" I asked.

"Sharing my knowledge with people is the most rewarding part of what I do, especially given the overwhelming number of animals who need our help. And every day when I take care of my own colony and interact with the cats, I'm reminded of why I've dedicated so much of my life to this program."

As I left, I told her that I felt that I had gotten so much from being a colony caretaker. She then shared with me a story of her own about Smoky the cat.

CHAPTER 11

Smoky

SMOKY IS A GRAY AND white cat who lived in an abandoned house near Jenny. She used to see him when she walked her dog, and she learned that the cat had belonged to a woman who'd once lived in the house and had passed away. The house had gone into foreclosure, but some of her nephews used to hang out on the porch and deal drugs. They were fairly rough characters who would occasionally yell at the cat and frighten him. But they also had a soft spot for their aunt's cat and would occasionally feed him.

Jenny saw that the cat wanted to stay in the area, so she put a shelter in the yard for him and fed him regularly. Smoky was an incredible rat catcher. There was a wood pile on the property, and Jenny would see him grabbing large rats out of the pile. Not every cat can go after the big rats, but Smoky was a pro. He would catch really big rats on a regular basis.

SMOKY LOSES HIS HOME

Unfortunately one day, the house where Smoky lived was sold. Jenny approached the new owner and asked him if she could continue to feed

Smoky. He told her that he did not want the cat in the area under any circumstances. Jenny tried to reason with him and explained that it would not cost him anything and that Smoky was a great rat catcher. The owner was unmoved and told her the cat had to go. Jenny asked for one week to trap and relocate Smoky. But she was unsure where to take him. He wasn't appropriate for Tree House because he was too aggressive. And he couldn't become part of an existing colony because he was a lone hunter.

Jenny remembered a man who had been asking for a feral cat—but he only wanted one. And he wanted a cat that could catch big rats. It was a match made in heaven. Jenny told Bill about Smoky, and he got to work building a cat shelter in his backyard. Bill had a large Irish Setter, so Jenny suggested that he construct a series of steps from the cat shelter to the top of a tall privacy fence so that Smoky would always have an easy way to get in and out of his area and wouldn't be frightened by the dog.

SMOKY'S NEW HOME

Smoky's cat shelter was incredible. It was a lovely green-and-white house that matched his owner's home down to the detail of the lattice work. And the backyard was a lovely, landscaped area with a pond replete with koi fish. Smoky made the transition and has flourished. He's much calmer, and he's caught plenty of big rats for Bill. The neighbors love him too. The neighbors on either side of Bill have places where he sits and visits with them. And they also feed him. Now Smoky has three places where he takes his meals and catnaps. Smoky went from being kicked out of the only home he ever knew to having three homes and three families who care about and love him.

And interestingly, the nephews ask about Smoky every time they see Jenny. Apparently, Smoky is a part of their aunt's legacy, and they are glad to hear that he is doing well. It's not something one would guess. But as I was learning, there were all sorts of unintended positive consequences to taking care of these cats.

CHAPTER 12

Duke

AS THE WINTER MONTHS PROGRESSED, I became less concerned about our cats. We had a regular feeding time, they were eating a good amount of cat food, and they looked like they had gained weight and were running around in the snow. All was well until the day that I saw that Duke had a wound on his side. I thought it was a bite wound because it was the size of a quarter. He was missing a patch of fur near his hind leg. I was feeding him when I saw it. It didn't look like he had received it that day—it looked a couple of days old. I was very upset to think that an animal had attacked him.

I talked to Jenny and Liz, and they said I should retrap him and bring him into the clinic, where they could take a look at him and also get his ear tipped (remove the top of his ear so he wouldn't be retrapped at any time in the future). I picked up a trap at Tree House and went to my home. I suddenly felt overwhelmed. How would I trap him? Would that cause him a lot of stress? What if he was okay and this step wasn't necessary?

I brought the trap down into their area, and as soon as one of the cats heard it, she bolted out of her sleeping shelter and ran as fast as she could out of the area. I felt terrible. So now I was stressing the other cats out, and I didn't have a clue about how to trap Duke.

I put the trap off to the side that afternoon and covered the top of it so the cats could get used to it. That night, I fed the cats and put a bowl of dry food in the cage and left it wired open. I went back inside and looked through the window. After a while, Duke jumped right into the cage and ate some of the dry food. When he was done, he jumped back out. We did this for three more meals, and each time Duke was the only one who jumped into the cage. I was beginning to think that this feat could be accomplished after all.

DUKE VISITS THE CLINIC

I was incredibly nervous the morning I had to get Duke to the clinic. I configured the trap so it would close once he stepped on a plate. I put the dry food in as I had before. When I brought the wet food down, he was already in the cage but the front hadn't shut. Apparently he hadn't stepped on the special plate. So when I put the food down, I shut the front. He kept on eating as if he didn't care.

After a while, I took him out of their area and carried him up into the house. He meowed loudly, and Eloise went to the bottom of the steps, stared at the cage, and watched me bring him into the house. Then both Allie and Eloise went to the sidewalk and looked into our side window. I don't want to anthropomorphize, but they seemed to be looking for Duke, and they seemed concerned.

Meanwhile, I put Duke into a spare bathroom and covered the cage. It was nice and warm in there, and he didn't make a sound. Then Liz came by to pick him up. As she left, both Allie and Eloise went to the front of the house and watched her take him away as he meowed loudly. It really seemed like they were worried. When I went downstairs to get their bowls, neither cat would get near me. When they saw me, they fled.

Duke went to the clinic, and I called the next day to see how he was doing and to find out what had bitten him. A lovely woman answered the phone and told me that Duke had not been bitten at all and that the wound on his side was some type of a skin infection. They had given Duke an antibiotic and treated the skin. Duke was fine. But there was one thing she had to tell me. Duke was not a male; *Duke was a female*!! So it turned out we had three female cats.

Liz brought Duke home from the clinic that day, and when she opened the trap, Duke bounded down the stairs to the other two cats. Eloise and Allie ran over to Duke, and the Rat Pack had a little reunion. First Eloise ran up to Duke, sniffed her, and then rubbed against her. Then Allie did the same thing. Soon the three of them were rubbing up against one another. The cats hadn't eaten much when Duke was gone, but they all ate a lot that night.

Duke

CHAPTER 13

Liz: A Study in Passion

I WANTED TO THANK LIZ for all she had done for us, so I offered to take her out to dinner a few days after she came back with Duke. We went to a local restaurant in my area, and I asked her how she had entered this line of work and what it was like. I was surprised to learn that she was an engineer by training and that she had been in the technical marketing profession for many years before she had started managing Community Cats.

Liz is an attractive woman with lovely, long hair and an infectious smile. The stories she told me that evening were definitely interesting. She had received an undergraduate degree in engineering and then an MBA at the University of Illinois. She eventually worked for a company in Chicago for over fifteen years as a product manager. Liz earned a good salary and would have stayed there indefinitely if the company had not let her go. Suddenly, she found herself without a job and a desire to do something different … But what?

Liz had been doing some volunteer work for Tree House for a couple of years. She's seen cats in her neighborhood and had been trapping them so they could be neutered and returned. The clinic employees and Jenny Schlueter were impressed by her zeal, so Jenny offered her a job as a Community Cats program manager. I wasn't clear what that job title actually meant, but I soon learned that it was a cross between a social worker, animal trapper, and community organizer. She currently works about sixty to sixty-five hours a week, and she works out of her home, her car, and the clinic that Tree House runs.

LIZ'S PROJECTS

She talked about her work in terms of "projects," which were colonies that had been identified by individuals in the community who had called Tree House for assistance. Sometimes it was huge colonies and sometimes it was a couple of kittens who had been dumped somewhere and would die if Liz didn't get to them in time. One of her first projects was a tip that came in about kittens in someone's yard. When Liz arrived there, she found seventeen kittens—four complete litters! It was a job that was overwhelming, so she immediately called for assistance from other trappers. They managed to get seventeen kittens and five adults trapped and neutered. Liz then found individuals to foster the kittens so they could be placed in homes. The adults were returned to their location, where they could live but no longer breed.

Liz explained to me that kittens are especially sweet but very fragile. Apparently, over half of kittens born outside will die before they're eight weeks old. They die from anemia, distemper, malnutrition, and mother cats abandoning them because they are unable to feed them or because they are too ill. Liz remembered the call she received from Garfield Park Conservatory, which is a common place for people to dump cats and kittens. Two kittens had been put into a flower pot outside the conservatory, and the staff called her as soon as they found them. Liz rushed over there, but it was too late for one of the kittens. The other kitten was put into a blanket on top of a Tupperware container filled with hot water, and Liz placed him on her lap and tried to keep him as warm as she could. He survived several months but died the week before our conversation. She was very sad as she relayed this to me.

DIFFICULT SITUATIONS: AN AUTO BODY BUSINESS GETS HEATED

The night we went to dinner was a tough one for Liz. She was dealing with two difficult neighbor situations. I was incredulous. A neighbor situation? Who could object to colony cats, I asked naively. All my neighbors ask me how the cats are on a regular basis. Today at the gym, a woman asked me about the program and thanked me for our contribution to the neighborhood. But that was not the case in the neighborhood where Liz had been that day. Apparently a hot dog business had sold its location to an auto body business. The hot dog business had always had feral cats on the premises and had fed them. When the owners sold their building, they never mentioned the cats to the new owners. And the new owners were furious. A passerby who had seen the cats called Tree House. The owners of the auto body wanted them removed immediately. In the middle of winter, it was impossible to trap, neuter, and relocate eleven cats. Liz was able to remove six kittens, but she didn't have a place for the other five cats, so she told the owners of the auto body shop it would take a few weeks to relocate them. The new owners told her that if she didn't get the cats out of there immediately, they would poison them or shoot them. Many neighbors in the area were feeding the cats, and the auto body employees were chasing the neighbors away and threatening them. One of the feeders was a retired Chicago cop whom they followed home and threatened. They kicked her front door, screaming and yelling. Their anger had no limits.

DIFFICULT SITUATIONS: A NEW CONDO OWNER

The other neighbor issue was also complicated. A colony caretaker was losing her home and had sold it in a short sale. The new owner didn't know there was a colony at the home, and she wanted to rent the property to tenants. She felt the colony would detract from the value of the property and would cause people with children to be less interested in it. Liz spent a great deal of time talking to the new owner and trying to figure out a solution. Even though people in the neighborhood would feed the cats going forward, the new owner wanted the cats out. Liz was faced with another relocation in the middle of winter, which was also impossible and inhumane, given that the cats were going to be outside in a cage for several weeks.

I was a little dumfounded as to why people disliked cats so much, and Liz explained that some of the colony caretakers were careless and allowed their cats to become a nuisance. It wasn't the cats' fault; it was the caretakers. If neighbors were unhappy about cats peeing in their yard, it was the caretaker's responsibility to get an outdoor litter box. Unfortunately, it's not always easy to do. Many of the people who feed cats are low income, so dealing with nuisance issues such as getting an outdoor litter box is extremely difficult. There are apparently "pet deserts," where you can't buy cat food and cat litter. And some of these people are not able to afford these things—Liz knows of several people who are literally going bankrupt feeding cats. I could see how feeding twenty cats and providing outdoor litter boxes could become very expensive.

The emotional nature of Liz's job became very apparent to me as we talked, and I finally asked the question that had been on my mind all night. "How are you able to cope with the long hours, all this responsibility, and the tremendous drama?"

"It's quite simple," she answered. "I really believe in what I'm doing. When you trap cats who are hungry, neuter them, get them vaccinated, and then put them in a good location, it's very fulfilling. And several of our colonies are ten years old. The cats are being well cared for and are thriving."

That's the life she's giving to them. I realized that she was changing the world one cat and one person at a time.

CHAPTER 14

Yvette: Changing Whole Neighborhoods

ANOTHER CARETAKER THAT I GOT in touch with was Yvette, who lives in Pilsen, a low-income area in Chicago. I headed over to meet her toward the end of winter 2013. Yvette lives in a house with a fenced-in yard that has several cat shelters around the perimeter of the yard. The day I visited, it was very cold, but I saw several members of her cat colony inside their heated shelters. Yvette has lived in that neighborhood since 2006, and she had a lot to say.

It all began with a dog. Yvette and her husband, Francisco, had done a service vacation for Best Friends Animal Society, where they took care of animals rather than going on a conventional vacation. While they were there, they bonded with a dog named Dundee Boy. Unfortunately, they lived in a condominium with a weight limit that Dundee Boy officially exceeded. They came back to Chicago and couldn't stop thinking about the dog. They thought about the fact that they wanted to eventually move out of their condo and have a house with a yard. So they bought a single-family house so they could adopt Dundee Boy. That was the home I visited that day.

FOURTEEN CATS IN THE YARD!

The first night the couple was in their new home, Yvette saw fourteen cats outside in her yard. She couldn't believe it. She offered them food and then called PAWS Chicago to ask for assistance. The person at PAWS was fairly short with Yvette on the phone and said the organization couldn't help her. So she started to blog about the cats in her yard. Another woman from PAWS called her a few weeks later and invited her in to talk about the cats. That's when she learned she needed to trap, neuter, and return them. The woman handed Yvette a humane trap.

"I was certainly not going to do that! I thought they were crazy," Yvette told me.

That was until she saw the first kitten. Winter was just starting, and she realized all of these cats in her yard were going to start having kittens. It would be a very rough winter for them, and she realized that her fourteen cats would soon become a much larger problem.

Yvette began trapping all the cats and having them spayed or neutered. It turned out that eight cats were very friendly, which became obvious after they had their surgeries, so she found them homes. The remaining six were clearly feral, and she returned them to her yard and continued to feed them. She particularly bonded with a large, black cat she named Amigo, a tabby she called Sam, and another tabby cat she named Tabitha.

As winter progressed, Yvette kept seeing a lot of cats around. She saw a lot of injured and sick cats and a lot of kittens. And at night, she heard cats yowling all the time, which is typically a mating call. It was difficult to sleep some nights because the noise was so loud.

YVETTE TAKES ON THE NEIGHBORHOOD

As a result of the number of cats who seemed to be in trouble, Yvette decided to go on a mission to help the other cats in her neighborhood. So she began trapping and fixing those cats as well. She estimated that the first year she had over fifty cats spayed or neutered in her neighborhood, which she did at her own cost (about $1,250).

She also tested every cat for feline leukemia and FIV+ status, which she also paid for out of her own pocket. FIV+ stands for feline immunodeficiency virus (FIV), which suppresses the immune system in cats and is similar to HIV in humans. Several of the cats in her yard and indoors are FIV+. It's not a death sentence, Yvette explained to me; cats can live long lives with FIV. It's transmitted through sex and very deep wounds that occur from fighting.

She remained committed to her mission. And the impressive thing is that, after the first couple of years, the neighborhood changed. The number of cats decreased, the number of sick and injured cats plummeted, and there were very few kittens. But more importantly, there was no howling at night. Suddenly, the neighborhood was more peaceful, with less noise and fewer cats.

Yvette also connected with other people who were feeding cats in the neighborhood and educated them about TNR and appropriate feeding. Some of the neighbors were feeding the neighborhood cats rice and beans, so she helped them understand that this diet wasn't good for cats. She also reached out to these other feeders and asked them to let her know if there were intact cats (in other words, cats who weren't neutered or spayed) running around. People in the neighborhood started alerting her to cats that needed to be fixed and began asking her if she could fix their house cats, which she did!

She told me that the social structure of cat communities is fairly complicated and that all the cats have very different personalities. Two dominant cats rule her yard—Golden Boy (aka Goldie) and Fred. Goldie is a male, and Fred is a female. Goldie and Fred decide which cats come into the yard, who eats there, how long they eat, and who can stay in the cat shelters. When there is enough food, they may let other neighborhood cats come in for a snack. But even when there is enough shelter, Goldie or Fred will send other cats out of the yard. Another cat who lives in the yard is Oreo. He's very close with Fred and acts as the welcoming committee there. If a new cat is in the yard, Oreo is usually hanging around with the newcomer.

SAD SAM

Yvette also told me that two of her feral cats have moved indoors, and their personalities are completely different inside. One of the cats who lives inside her home is called Sam. She and her husband used to call him Sad Sam because he always seemed to have a sad look on his face. He would never let humans touch him when he was outside. He was a tough cat, and he bossed Goldie and the other cats around the yard. One day, Yvette drove into the alley to feed some of the cats there. She got out of her car and inadvertently left her door open. When she returned, Sam was in the passenger seat. She had been feeding him in her yard for a year, and she wasn't quite sure what to do. She drove around to her home, and her husband came out with a cat carrier, which they put in the backseat. When Yvette touched Sam, he didn't resist her. Then she picked him up and put him in the carrier. She noticed he was very stiff. He was definitely asking for help. They took him to the vet and learned that he had several abscessed teeth and was dehydrated and weak. Yvette and Francisco nursed Sam back to health in their home for several weeks. When he was feeling better, he began asking to go back outside. After a while, he stopped asking.

When I saw Sam at Yvette's house, he was very lovable and sat next to me for much of our conversation. He rubbed against me and wanted to be petted by a complete stranger. I was absolutely amazed that Sam had once been a feral cat. Although Sam was tough outside the home, he was a complete sweetheart inside. And every summer, Yvette allows all the cats to meet through an outdoor enclosure called a catio, which is on the front of her house. It allows the indoor cats to be outside without any danger. When Sam goes into that space, there is a big reunion in the backyard. Goldie will come over, and they will sniff and rub each other in a sweet way. It is clear that they recognize and are glad to see one another.

I asked Yvette about how dogs and cats relate, given that she has dogs in her house, and she told me the story of Tabitha and Dundee Boy.

Sam

Oreo

CHAPTER 15

Tabitha and Dundee Boy

DUNDEE BOY WAS A CHOW chow-Australian shepherd mix whom Yvette and Francisco adopted. He was a fluffy black-and-tan dog with lovely, thick fur who had lived for five years at a shelter before they met him on their service vacation. Tabitha was a feral cat in Yvette's yard. When the two animals first met one another, Tabitha ran away in fear. And Dundee Boy had been described in his adoption papers as a dog who didn't like cats. But somehow things changed.

Yvette first started noticing the connection between the two animals when Tabitha would come to the outside of her house and stare into her window. At first she thought that Tabitha was looking for food. She wasn't; she was looking for Dundee Boy. And Dundee Boy often looked for Tabitha. When he saw her out in the yard, he would often get very excited and bark until they let him go out.

Dundee Boy would go out in the yard where Tabitha was waiting. They would walk around the yard, play, and nuzzle one another. When Yvette and Francisco would take Dundee Boy for a walk, Tabitha would often accompany them. She never let them touch her, but she would let Dundee Boy get close to her and nuzzle her. And when Dundee Boy got into the car to go somewhere, Tabitha would often look longingly after him.

TABITHA GETS SICK

About a year after the two met, Tabitha got sick. She began to lose weight. She would rush to the food bowl when there was food in it, but she wouldn't eat. Yvette knew that she and Francisco had to do something, so they devised a way to capture Tabitha in their entrance hallway. They took her to the vet, and she was diagnosed with giardia, which required twenty-one days of medication. Yvette realized that the only way they could save Tabitha's life was to keep her in a spare bedroom and administer the daily medication. That was going to be very difficult, given that Tabitha was used to being outside and was extremely fearful of people. She would not let them get near her.

The first time Yvette and Francisco tried to give Tabitha her medication, she fought them with a ferocity that surprised them. They were unsure whether they would be able to save her, until they brought Dundee Boy in to visit her. When Dundee Boy was with her, Tabitha relaxed, and she let the humans give her the medication. And then she and Dundee Boy snuggled. Eventually, she even let Yvette pet her, but only when Dundee Boy was present. Otherwise, she was nervous and scared.

After twenty-one days, Tabitha regained her health, and Yvette made the decision to keep her inside with Dundee Boy. The two animals enjoyed many snuggles and playtimes together. It was a happy arrangement until Dundee Boy died in 2011. He had bloat and went to the veterinarian for surgery but passed away during the procedure. When he didn't return, Tabitha howled for weeks. She was devastated. It broke Yvette and Francisco's hearts. It was a very difficult time for all of them, but they managed to eventually cope and adjust to the change. When I went to visit them, Tabitha was still living indoors, and although she has had many opportunities to go outside, she has decided to live indoors. Yvette says that Tabitha is very sweet and friendly to them but is nervous around new people. But more importantly, she is a happy, healthy cat these days.

Tabitha and Dundee Boy

CHAPTER 16

Out on the Streets with Erica

I STARTED TO WONDER ABOUT the history of my cats, so I asked Liz if she knew where they had come from. She explained that her colleague Erica had handled that situation. Erica is a Community Cats program director at Tree House, and she does many of the things that Liz does but in different locations of the city. She humanely traps cats, has them spayed or neutered, and then relocates them or returns them to their original location. I was intrigued to meet Erica because she knew about my cats and because I was curious about what exactly she did, so I asked to accompany her on one of her "projects."

I met Erica over in a Polish neighborhood on the north side of Chicago. She is a petite, dark-haired woman with a strong voice, a forceful personality, and a dry wit. She is known at Tree House for coming up with funny names for things and for generally seeing the humorous side of life. I met her in front of a large, older home where she explained that this project was similar to many of the ones she handles on a regular basis. Erica pulled humane traps out of her car as she told me that we were helping a woman named Mary who owned the three-story building facing the street but who lived in the coach house in the back. Mary was renting the front building, but very few of her tenants were actually paying their rent. Just then, I heard a woman yelling from the coach house followed by a door slamming, and I saw a cat running out of the house. The woman was Mary.

TRAPPING CATS IN FREEZING TEMPERATURES FOR MARY

Mary is an elderly Polish woman who had started feeding feral cats on her porch. Soon a couple cats turned into fifteen cats, as they started to reproduce. When we arrived at the front door, Mary told me in broken English that "Mama cat" needed to stop having kittens and that all the cats in the yard were Mama's offspring. It had to stop, she reiterated. She was a plump woman in her seventies dressed in a pink housecoat, she had very few teeth, her hair was in disarray, and she looked completely overwhelmed.

We stepped into her kitchen, which reeked of cat urine, and I was surprised to see several feral cats. I asked her how that situation had occurred, and she explained that, when the cats get cold they, ask to come inside. I tried to get within a few feet of one of the cats, and it ran into the bathroom. These cats were not semiferal; they were fully feral.

Our task that night was to trap any cats that were intact, particularly "Mama cat," and to take them to the clinic to be spayed or neutered. Mary was able to get several cats inside her house by the scruffs of their necks, and she forcefully put them into the traps. We also set several traps around the outside of her home and on her front porch, but the cats who went into the cages had already been fixed, so we let them go.

We would set traps, leave the area, and then sit in the car and wait. It was brutally cold that night (about 10 degrees Fahrenheit), so by the time we had been out to check the traps and make sure they were working, our fingers and toes were numb. We went back and forth several times that night because, Erica explained, she did not want any cat sitting in a trap in the cold weather for more than twenty minutes.

Every time we went from Erica's car to the coach house, we ended up checking in with Mary. Every interaction with her pulled at my heart strings. She told me that she was losing her home and that she had hired a lawyer who had cheated her out of a lot of money. She would rant for a bit, and then she would begin asking about a cat that had been taken from her home to get medical care that she could not afford. It was deaf and blind. She would start to cry and ask for this particular cat. It became clear to me that Mary was completely overwhelmed by her life and by the cat situation. Erica was obviously providing an invaluable service to this woman.

As Erica and I sat in the car, I asked about my colony's history. She told me that that the Rat Pack came from a large colony where they had been kept in large cages. None of them were spayed or neutered, and the colony kept getting larger and larger. Then the group started to get sick. The couple that was taking care of them didn't believe in medical care for religious reasons, so it was a horrendous situation. Erica intervened and pulled the cats out of there. She spayed or neutered all of them and then tried to get as many kittens adopted as possible. Duke was one of the few kittens whom they could not get fostered, so she remained with the group until she was relocated to my home.

A ONE-YEAR ANNIVERSARY

That night was Erica's one-year anniversary, and she reflected on the last twelve months. She said that her work was exhausting, that she was often subject to harassment from people who didn't understand what she was doing, and that her husband often worried about her safety. She said the job was intense and that she had lost twenty-five pounds in the last year. I learned that she was very educated; she had two master's degrees in archeology. And she told me that this job was the toughest one she'd ever held. She told me that trapping cats comprises about 15 percent of what she does and the rest of the time she is largely talking to people, educating them, and helping people in difficult situations.

"So many people need help. I get calls at all hours of the day and night, sometimes from people who are frantic. And almost every person I've helped continues to call me for various reasons; they need food for their cats, one of the cats is sick, the neighbors are complaining, there are more cats on the property who need to be fixed, the alderman has called and said to stop feeding, they've been fined, and lots of other reasons," she told me.

In one case, a woman called Erica absolutely hysterical because a neighbor was threatening to poison her feral cat colony. Erica rushed over to the area and was able to save a couple of the cats, but the rest of them had been poisoned. It was heartbreaking.

I asked how common these types of situations are, and she said that they are infrequent but they do occur. Some people don't like cats. She said that, in some cases, neighbors are taking colony cats and driving them to other areas of the city to get rid of them. They have found cats many miles away, and it's clear the cat didn't get there without assistance. However, she said that, with all of the challenges, she sees so many great people doing wonderful things for cats and many colonies where the caretakers and neighbors are working together.

We finally left Mary's house with four of her feral cats, including Mama cat. We had one black one, two black-and-white ones, and a gray one. At the clinic, I gave them each a name for their paperwork—Vincent, Soprano, Concierge, and Charcoal.

As we were getting finished, Liz pulled up to the clinic with seventeen cats that she and several volunteers had humanely trapped that night. The next day was National Spay Day, and the volunteers were out in force to try to meet Tree House's goal of spaying or neutering sixty cats. Liz was going out the next morning to the same location to trap more feral cats and said I could tag along.

CHAPTER 17

Liz and National Spay Day

LIZ AND I STARTED OUT early the next morning and drove to a neighborhood a few miles from O'Hare Airport. It was really cold—about 20 degrees Fahrenheit. We were meeting another volunteer who had been part of the group that had trapped at that area the night before. We rolled into an area where there was a mixture of homes and businesses. As we drove down an alley, I saw several businesses on the right and several homes on the left side.

A HUGE COLONY IN A TERRIBLE SITUATION

We parked in a lot behind a tavern where an older couple had been feeding feral cats. Several makeshift cat shelters sat haphazardly at the back of the building, empty dishes interspersed among them. When we walked toward the building, two scruffy cats ran out of the area and into a neighbor's backyard. We walked up onto the top deck, and it was covered with cat feces. It was awful.

On the left-hand side of the alley there was a pile of junk. A closer examination revealed some cardboard boxes and other items that were functioning as cat shelters, along with some empty bowls and plates. This area was also a place where cats were living. When we went to place traps in that area, a large black cat wandered out of a shelter and crossed the alley.

Liz explained that there were several feeders in the area and that a few cats had reproduced and turned into about sixty feral cats. Liz had been slowly educating the people in the area about TNR and how they needed to trap, neuter, and then return or relocate the cats. Tree House also registered a couple of feeders to be caretakers of the colony. But it was a major problem. And there was animosity between neighbors. Some of the neighbors didn't like the makeshift shelters, which were an eyesore, and they didn't want the large number of feral cats walking around. I was pretty sympathetic to them when I saw the situation.

We set the traps behind the tavern and next to the junk pile, but there were no takers that morning. The remaining members of the colony were probably frightened from the night before, and the food we used in the trap froze quickly and may not have been appetizing. It was also possible that someone had fed them before we got there, so they might not have been hungry. However, in between checking traps, we wandered over to the veterinary clinic that was a couple doors down from the banquet hall to let them know what we were doing.

A VISIT WITH THE LOCAL VETERINARIAN

We walked into the main office of the clinic, and Liz introduced us and explained why we were there. The manager of the veterinary clinic was happy to hear about our efforts and said that she would gladly fix any male cats we found (for free) and that she was in full support of the TNR program. She explained that having the colony in the alley was a very difficult situation for them. Cats were getting run over in the alley and kittens were being brought in who were very sick. At least a few cats had been brought in who were missing their legs after getting hit by cars. One cat had been hit and had to have his legs amputated. After they treated the cat, the veterinary tech had adopted it. But she knew the bigger problem was the large number of cats reproducing and the inadequate housing for them.

Liz told the veterinary manager that she had trapped seventeen cats the night before and that we would clean up the area and put in proper shelters for the cats. The new shelters would protect the cats from the cold, and the area would look much better. The manager of the clinic said that she would be willing to have a meeting with the neighbors to discuss the situation and educate them about TNR. She realized that this problem was going to require the community coming together. It was very encouraging to me to see how everyone was pitching in to help.

NATIONAL SPAY DAY AT TREE HOUSE

We left the area and went over to the Tree House clinic to see National Spay Day in action. When we arrived, sixty-two cats were waiting to be neutered or spayed, and I could feel a tremendous energy around the clinic. The Tree House clinic in Bucktown is a relatively small space with a small waiting area, two operating rooms, several rooms to hold cats, and a break area for the volunteers and employees. One full-time veterinarian, who specializes in spaying and neutering, is on staff. Over half of the procedures are done for feral cats.

Tree House's staff had set the goal to spay or neuter sixty cats in honor of the day and were thrilled that they had exceeded their goal. When we arrived, there were people in every room, and each person had a role in the process. One person was preparing the cats, veterinarians were conducting surgeries in both operating rooms, and others was watching each of the cats who had just undergone surgery to ensure they were doing well. The atmosphere was busy and happy. And the Tree House folks were proud that they had reached their goal.

One thing I learned that day was that many veterinarians are not used to treating feral cats and don't understand what to do with them. It's a major problem. A feral cat must be contained in a humane cage and will require sedation before it can be removed from the cage, due to its fear of humans. Many vets aren't used to this procedure, and some will encourage caretakers to put feral cats down simply because they're feral. It's very unfortunate. I made a note at that point to call my regular vet to ask if she could treat my colony cats.

THE HUMANE SOCIETY OF THE US

That day, all the surgeries were paid for by the Humane Society of the United States. I sat with the representative from that organization, Annette Bellezzo, and we talked about the problems of getting people to spay and neuter their pets. She said that many people don't get their pets fixed for many reasons. Some people don't have money, and others don't have transportation. Others just aren't aware of the necessity and importance of getting pets fixed.

The Humane Society has a program that sends people out to educate the American public about the importance of spaying or neutering, and the organization pays for surgeries and provides transportation if it's needed. I was very impressed. I had no idea that there were such programs out there. Annette said that many people in low-income areas where financial resources are stressed need this kind of help. I was about to see that principle in action with my next visit to a colony caretaker in Humboldt Park.

CHAPTER 18

Jennie and the Neighborhood Cats

I WENT TO VISIT JENNIE in Humboldt Park, which is a low-income area of Chicago. There were several abandoned houses that were boarded up near her home and an abandoned building across the street. This area clearly wasn't thriving economically. Jennie is a trained painter with a master's degree in fine arts who has lived in Humboldt Park for the past twenty years. She moved there because it was the place she could afford as a single mother with a limited income.

ABANDONED AND FERAL CATS

Jennie told me that abandoning cats in her neighborhood is not unusual and that people often get kittens believing they will be able to hunt for their own food when they become adults. Spaying and neutering cats is also less common and not a priority when people have limited resources and do not understand the number of kittens who are born every year.

As a result, she has adopted several stray cats who were abandoned in Humboldt Park. One cat, Chow Down, had been left behind when its owners moved because they mistakenly believed that cats are more attached to places than people. Chow Down went methodically from house to house looking for food and a place to live. When he got to Jennie's house, her son gave him some tuna fish casserole, and he never left.

Taking care of feral cats started later. In 2010, Jennie found a litter of kittens in her garage, and she contacted Tree House to get help, which is how she became aware of the TNR program. She got the cats fixed, and they became her garage colony. Then she and several volunteers from Tree House went and trapped, neutered, and then returned many of the feral cats in her neighborhood. The impact has been tremendous. Jennie is seeing fewer cats, fewer sick cats, and fewer kittens.

CARING FOR SEVERAL COLONIES

Jennie is one of a few colony caretakers in Humboldt Park, and she currently takes care of three major colonies. She took me on her route, which was impressive. She had set up feeding stations near buildings that have been abandoned, and she calls all the cats by name. We arrived when it was not the regular feeding time; she called out each cat's name, and they came running! They clearly knew her voice and understood that it was time to eat. Several of the cats whom we fed that day are "owned" but are not fed by their owners, so Jennie takes care of them.

I had to ask. "Why do you do all of this? It's clearly expensive and very time-consuming to feed all these cats."

"Because I can sleep at night knowing the cats are taken care of—getting regular vaccines, getting regular food, and having places to sleep," she said without hesitation.

It also gives her an important focus for her life.

"When I had to leave my job as a school teacher because of an accident on the job, I fell into a major depression and had trouble getting out of bed. It's very difficult to work your entire life and have nothing to do. It's devastating to be injured and unable to do much. The money I would have spent on antidepressants gets spent on cat food."

She also gets out of the house, gets regular exercise several times a day, and is connecting with people in her area.

The neighborhood clearly values what she does, which I witnessed firsthand. Several neighbors we ran into on her feeding route talked with her about the cats and asked about any colony cats that they hadn't seen recently. She is well-known in the neighborhood, and before I left, she related a touching story.

"At one point, I was walking on an icy sidewalk, and I slipped and fell. My son was nearby, as well as two pretty tough drug dealers. The drug dealers rushed over to help me up. They told my son, 'We take care of her because she takes care of the cats in our neighborhood.'"

Yellow Boy—One of Jennie's Colony Cats

Coco—One of Jennie's Colony Cats

CHAPTER 19

Stigma, Silence, and Katie

THAT FEBRUARY, I WENT TO a Mardi Gras party that Katie, a good friend, was having at her home. While I was there, I mentioned my cat colony to her, and she said that she had one too. I couldn't believe it. I have been to her house many times, she has been to mine, we have gone to dinner many times, and we attend a book club together. I was shocked.

"You have to tell me all about it," I said.

She had a few hurricane drinks in her and was more than happy to talk.

GUESTS AT THE BACK DOOR

It all started several years ago, when Katie was a professional writer living with her mother and aunt. She was writing for a cooking blog and was making chicken when she heard a banging on her back door. She went to the door, but was no one there. So she went back to the stove and heard the banging again. But once again, no one was at the door.

By the time she heard the banging for the third time, she was concerned that she was losing her mind, until she looked down and saw two calico kittens on the doorstep. They were playing and were bumping into the back door. She didn't even think twice about going into the kitchen and shredding some of the chicken for them. They devoured it.

The next day, the two kittens came back to her doorstep with their mother and another kitten, so Katie fed them again. These feedings occurred for the next few days, so she told her family what she was doing to get their reaction to the situation. Everyone thought that it was fine. She had no long-term plan, but she bought the cats a shelter to live in, fed them regularly, and started blogging about her experience. After she had been blogging for a few weeks, a friend of hers told her about TNR and how she should try to trap, neuter, and return the cats to her yard. She liked this idea and got in touch with Tree House to get some humane traps.

THE FAMILY GETS FIXED

Getting the cat family spayed and neutered turned out to be quite challenging. The original calico kittens disappeared, and Katie learned that they had been adopted by someone in the neighborhood. But the mother and the other kitten, Basil, were eating regularly. Katie managed to get Basil fixed, but the mother cat, Margo, was extremely difficult to trap. And then she started to look bigger. She was clearly pregnant. After a couple of months, she disappeared for a few days and then showed up much smaller. Margo continued to feed regularly but didn't bring her four new kittens around until they were about six weeks old. Margo moved her kittens around every few days until they got old enough to stay in the family shelter that Katie had bought for them.

After the kittens were weaned, Katie got them spayed or neutered, but the mother cat was extremely difficult to catch. When they finally trapped her, she panicked and howled loudly in the cage. The kittens were nearby and rushed to the cage that contained their mother. They were crying in response to her panic and were all clearly upset. It was very difficult taking Margo to get spayed that day. As she howled in the backseat of her car, Katie couldn't do anything to reassure her. "This is hard, and it takes courage to do this," she told me.

Margo was returned to her kittens a day later, and they had a sweet reunion. She was also a changed cat. Perhaps the change was due to the surgery or the experience of getting trapped, or both. She became more easygoing and would allow Katie and her family to get close to her and touch her. Before the surgery, she would wince if they touched her, but afterward, she was much calmer and much more affectionate.

STRONG BONDS

The cat family has stayed together, and they are very attached to one another. They don't leave the yard much and are generally together as a group. They don't fight and often look out for each other. When the kittens started to eat solid food, the older brother cat, Basil, would ensure that his younger siblings wouldn't fall off the porch when they ate. He would put himself at the end of the porch and nudge them away if they got too close.

So why the silence? Why had Katie never shared this part of her life with me? We surmised that the topic had never come up, but many colony caretakers are surprisingly silent about their activities—in part because of the stigma associated with being a "cat lady."

"Some people's eyes start to roll when you tell them what you're doing, and they look at you as if you're odd. Many caretakers worry about their cats being taken away or about someone trying to hurt them. In our case, a neighbor who gets upset about really minor things came over one day asking about the cats. I just avoided her question. I worry she will try to get the cats removed. You love your cats, so you don't say anything, to protect them," she explained.

We talked about why some people don't like cats, and Katie mused that it may be because people don't really understand cats and may feel rejected by them.

"Cats are more aware of their vulnerabilities than dogs, so they're more fearful and less outgoing in their affection. They're also more likely to scratch and bite if threatened. Perhaps early experiences as a child have ingrained an attitude of dislike," she said.

I thought her explanation made sense and could explain gender differences in cat ownership. Little girls may be gentler and more patient with cats than little boys, who are highly active and less-well-suited for an animal that is inherently fearful.

Katie has since moved out of her mother's home but goes back twice a week to take care of the cats. What had started out as an independent venture has become a family affair, and each member of the family takes turns feeding and caring for the little colony.

"It's brought the family closer together, and we do things for one another through the animals. I'm a very independent person, and there isn't much you can do for me. But taking care of the cats is one of the things that my mother and aunt do for me," she said.

"What else have you learned from the experience?" I asked.

Katie thought about it for a moment and then replied, "Patience. Cats have their own timetable, and gaining a cat's trust is a slow process. You have to let them come to that place on their own, and you have to be patient. But it's well worth it when they run up to you and want to be petted and loved."

CHAPTER 20

Howard and Cats Actually at Work

ONE OF THE MORE INTERESTING colony caretakers I met was Howard Skolnik, owner of a highly specialized steel-drum manufacturing company on the southwest side of Chicago. I went over to see Skolnik Industries to learn what role feral cats can play for a manufacturer.

Howard is a high-energy person who is passionate about many things. When you go into his office, you will see an eclectic mixture of possessions. Each one has a story. To the right of his desk are steel drums that were made into chairs by his son, Sasha. They're surprisingly comfortable. On his wall is a twisted bit of glass and metal, which looks like a piece of modern art, but it's actually the remains of a skylight that was destroyed when a major fire swept through his factory in 1987. Howard was determined to rebuild his business, which he did, and he now has over a hundred employees. After talking with him, you understand that he has a steely determination, great passion, and a calmness that's unusual.

CONSTRUCTION AND RATS

Feral cats came into Howard's life when he decided to do some construction on his building, and the work disturbed an underground network of rats. He had never seen rats in the area, but all of a sudden, he began seeing them quite a bit. He didn't want to use rat poison because rats eat it and then go into the walls of a building and die. The result is a terrible stench that requires opening the walls to remove dead rats. He also wanted to do something that was more environmentally friendly. He was talking about the issue with a friend, Maureen Duffy, who at the time was working with Tree House. She suggested feral cats as the answer to his problem.

Howard and Maureen got in touch with Jenny Schlueter, who had some feral cats that needed a new home because their caretaker had just passed away. The folks at Skolnik built a large (eight foot by four foot by four foot) cat condo, and Jenny brought over two cats, whom they named Prince and King. The cats were incredibly fearful and aggressive whenever anyone got near them.

After a couple of months in the cat condo, Prince and King were let out into the main floor of the facility, and they got right to work. They patrol an area that is sixty-five thousand square feet. The facility is impressive. The company produces a multitude of drums in an eight-hour shift. When I was there, all lines were in operation, and I watched sheets of carbon steel become welded and formed into drums and get painted right before my eyes. The facility has doors and large loading docks that are open to the outside. It would be very easy for a rat to enter. But there were none, Howard told me. Prince and King were doing an excellent job keeping them away and getting rid of any that wandered inside.

ROYALTY AT SKOLNIK INDUSTRIES

We went to go see Prince and King, who are cream-colored cats and live in the cat condo located in a quiet corner of the facility, complete with ramps and places to sleep during the day. They tend to go out into the facility at night when no one is around. When we arrived at their habitat, they were napping, but they both came out. They have gone from being fearful and aggressive to being very sweet. They came up to Howard, and he petted each one. King went out and sat among some black drums and watched me from a distance. Prince nuzzled up to Howard and eventually came over to me. It was clear they were a lot less feral then they had been when they'd first arrived.

"So what is the effect of having cats on the premises?" I asked.

"It sends a number of messages about the company. The fact that we invested in a nontoxic solution tells employees that the company wants to provide a healthy, clean place to work. It also says that the company is progressive and willing to try innovative solutions."

"But do employees ever complain about the cats or have issues with cat allergies?"

He laughed and said, "We have to discourage employees from spending too much time with the cats. We also have to discourage people from feeding them because we kept finding empty cans of cat food around their quarters. Employees were sneaking food to them."

"What about customers? Does it matter to them?" I asked.

"It does. Whenever I give a tour of the facility, I always ask customers if they like cats. If they do, I show them our setup for Prince and King."

Clearly they believe it makes a difference to customers because the Cats at Work program is described on their website under the heading "Why Skolnik?"

As I left, Howard told me, "At Skolnik, everyone has a job to do, and Prince and King are part of the Skolnik team. They may not get paid in cash, but they do get a nice place to live, lots of food, and great care. And the employees are very fond of their four-legged coworkers."

Prince

King

CHAPTER 21

Virginia and the Office Cats

ANOTHER CARETAKER I TALKED TO who had cats in the workplace was Virginia Carstarphen, who owns the restaurant Trader Todd's and the Chicago Inn, a ten-room bed-and-breakfast in Lakeview. I called Virginia to learn about her experiences as a colony caretaker, and she began by telling me that her involvement with feral cats and Tree House started when her brother came to visit.

A CHANCE ENCOUNTER WITH A FERAL FAMILY

Virginia was taking her brother to the train station when a cat ran in front of her car and darted across Sedgwick to the 18th District Police Station. After dropping her brother off at the station, she came back to the area and found the cat and her three kittens hiding under some bushes. She brought back some food to feed the young family and then started to think about how to help them. She started calling everyone she knew to see if they could assist her with the feral cats. Very few people even returned her calls. She realizes now that it was because people are overwhelmed with the stray cat situation in Chicago and don't know what to do in these circumstances.

The one person who did call her back was Andrea Goldberg, who was working with an organization called Furry Friends, then located in the building that now houses the Tree House Bucktown clinic. (Furry Friends is no longer in existence.) Andrea got someone from Furry Friends to come out and trap the cat family. All three kittens were adopted, and the mother cat was eventually placed in a shelter.

CATS WORKING IN THE BEER GARDEN

As a result of this experience, Virginia became interested in helping other feral and stray cats. When she would see an animal that needed help, she would pick it up and call the various animal organizations in the city to see who could assist. When her husband, Todd, learned about the Cats at Work program he wanted to become a colony caretaker. Their restaurant was located next to a derelict building, and the alley was often filled with rats. It was a miserable situation. Todd and Virginia got in touch with Jenny Schlueter at Tree House, and she set them up with a colony of three cats.

They set up the colony at the back of the beer garden in a heated storage shed. Virginia assumed the cats would come out at night and wouldn't interact with people in the garden. However, the staff at the restaurant was very interested in the cats and began interacting with them almost immediately. One of the cats had an autoimmune disease, and it died shortly after its arrival, but the other two cats thrived. One was a female named Eula May, and the other was a male named Mr. Sherbert, who was an orange cat. The two cats had very different personalities. Eula May was very shy and fearful, whereas Mr. Sherbert was more outgoing and curious.

Over the course of the next few months, the cats interacted more and more with the employees and the patrons of the restaurant. Mr. Sherbert was particularly social and would often sit on the windowsills and look into the restaurant while people were eating and drinking. And over time, he became interested in watching basketball games on TV. Whenever there was a game on, he would sit at the window and watch the entire game. Apparently, he is a big Bulls fan, Virginia joked. He still watches basketball games to this day.

Over time, Mr. Sherbert became more comfortable, and he wandered into the restaurant. It took a while to corral him. And then he wandered over to the neighbor's yard, where there was a collection of pet bunnies in a cage. Mr. Sherbert was very interested in the bunnies, and Virginia knew that the neighbor wouldn't be happy if something happened to their bunnies. So, she decided it was time for the cats to come live inside.

A NEW HOME

But where should the cats go? Virginia and her husband already had two cats in their small apartment, and they didn't want to have four cats in a small space. So they decided to install Eula May and Mr. Sherbert in their office where they run their two businesses. Several employees work in the office, and they've all really enjoyed having the two cats around. The cats have now lived inside for four years.

"Are there are issues having cats in the office? I'm having visions of a cat walking on a keyboard and an e-mail being sent out with gibberish," I said.

"You might expect things like that to happen, but it's very rare to find things knocked over or disturbed. And we put our keyboards on the tops of our computers when we aren't at our desks so we never have any problems with cats typing."

Apparently, the cats like living in the office and have become very close to each other over time. Mr. Sherbert still goes out exploring on a regular basis. Sometimes he leaves the office and goes downstairs.

Eula May will always wait patiently at the office door for him to return. Virginia says he is Eula May's hero. And when he comes back, she snuggles up with him on an office chair.

A LASTING IMPACT

"So how has this experience and how have the cats affected you?" I asked.

"They are a reminder of how precious life is for all of us. These are creatures who might have been thrown away or forgotten, and they somehow found us. And I've learned some valuable lessons along the way. I've learned to have patience and not to have expectations about how animals will behave or how they will develop. You have to let them become what they will become."

Virginia has continued to save stray and feral cats in Chicago and in Detroit, where she and her husband often go for business. She said that Tree House helps her with any cats she finds, and she fosters cats for them in return. She's been so impressed with the organization that she holds several fundraisers for them, including a Meow Luau and Fat Cat Tuesday. And she and Todd donate a percentage of the sales from their veggie burgers at Trader Todds to Tree House. I was impressed that a small business like hers was doing so much for Tree House.

"So do you think you'll have another feral cat colony?" I asked.

"We probably will, but not in the beer garden. I'm currently working with my church, Lakeview Lutheran, and they will be putting a feral cat colony on their grounds. My pastor, Liala Buekema, and a parishioner, Danielle Mintzlaff, are going to have a colony that the homeless kids in the area will help care for. They can learn firsthand about responsibility and caring for another creature."

It's a great lesson for all of us.

CHAPTER 22

Dean: The Reluctant Caregiver

THE LAST CARETAKER I TALKED to was Dean, who lives in Portage Park. Dean is a man in his late sixties who has spent his entire life in Chicago. He currently lives in the family home where he grew up as a child. He has never been on an airplane and has never traveled much.

"I just don't have a need. I love Chicago," he said.

After going to college, he taught in the Chicago public school for several years and eventually became a forklift operator at McCormick Place, where he was a teamster. He is a regular guy in some ways and is completely unique in other ways. When you talk to him, he will impress you with his positive outlook on life. He's still trying to learn new things, trying to overcome bad habits, and trying to have a rich life. He has many friends and lots of activities, including creating a following on Twitter. You get the strong impression that his life is getting better every year.

"I DON'T LOVE OR HATE CATS"

When I sat down with him, he told me, "I don't love or hate cats."

Now I was curious. As a colony caretaker, I can attest to the amount of work and the degree of dedication it takes. I had become attached to my cats through the many months I had been taking care of them.

"How did someone who doesn't love cats become involved in such an endeavor?" I asked.

"About ten years ago, a couple of cats moved into my garage. I didn't think too much of it until two cats became fifteen cats. I wasn't sure what to do."

He talked to a few people about the problem. He even thought about rounding up the cats and taking them out to a forest preserve, but a neighbor told him that was essentially giving them a death sentence. One person offered to poison them, but he was aghast at the idea. He reiterated to me that, although he doesn't love cats, they are living creatures and he couldn't kill them either purposefully or inadvertently. "It would be wrong," he told me.

TREE HOUSE PROVIDES ASSISTANCE

He was talking to a friend, Marci Bloodworth, about the situation, and she referred him to Tree House. Liz Houtz came over to assess the situation. Together they trapped all fifteen cats, had them neutered or spayed, and returned the feral ones to his backyard. The friendly ones and the kittens were adopted. Liz taught Dean how to take care of the cats, and she built him a "cat motel," which he installed in his garage. They also cut a hole on the side of his garage so the cats would have an accessible, safe entryway to their living area.

The colony now comprises six to eight cats whom Dean feeds regularly. It was feeding time while I was there, and three shy cats came out but refused to approach their feeding bowl while we were standing there.

One of them was a light-orange-colored cat, another one was a gray tabby, and the third one was black. They were clearly well-fed and healthy. But they were completely feral and would not approach us. When I went near their area, one of them shot into another yard. I looked at the cats through a window on Dean's back porch, and he told me a little about each one. "The light-orange one was born on my front porch and is very timid," he said.

NEIGHBORS AND THE VACUUM EFFECT

One of the interesting things Dean revealed involved his neighbors. Apparently, several neighbors are also feeding the cats. He said he regularly finds empty plates of food near his garage, and he knows that a nearby neighbor feeds the cats when they come down to her home. Dean's cats have actually become the neighborhood cats, and several people are watching over them and feeding them these days.

"What would have happened if the cats had been removed?" I asked.

"It's likely that other cats would have moved into the area and that I would have been back where I started. You know, my colony keeps to itself and doesn't let other cats into their territory, so I have pretty much the same cats there all the time."

Dean essentially explained the vacuum effect, which has been documented by cat researchers. Whenever there is a food source, cats will move into that area and feed there. If you remove a colony of feral cats, new feral cats will move right in. Through TNR, the colonies stay with the food source and slowly stabilize the population given their natural territoriality.

"So what do you get out of this experience?" I wondered.

"I get peace of mind. I know I've done the right thing. It was my responsibility, and I stepped up to it. I look out onto my backyard, and I know that the cats enjoy playing and hanging out back there."

I looked into his backyard and saw many tree stumps to perch on and lots of places to hide. I realized that, although he didn't love cats, he was taking good care of them.

I left wishing there were more people in the world like Dean.

CHAPTER 23

Cats in the 47th Ward

FERAL CAT COLONIES WERE POPPING up in different areas of Chicago, but one place where they were being promoted was in the 47th Ward. In this ward, a progressive alderman by the name of Ameya Pawar had been open to hearing about a program called Cats at Work. The program had been suggested by one of his employees, Dara Salk, who had been helping to trap, neuter, and return feral cats on the south side. When she happened on the idea of relocating cats to her ward to deal with a rat problem, a major light bulb went off.

"It's absolutely brilliant! It's a win for the ward, a win for the caretakers, and a win for the cats!" she exclaimed.

I went over to meet Dara in her office to learn more about how the program was working out for them. Dara is a woman who has lots of energy when she talks. She's extremely proud of her ward, the alderman, and the many programs they spearhead. And she absolutely glows when she talks. And after spending an hour with her, I was pretty sure that all social problems can be solved.

A "HOUSE PROUD" WARD

The 47th Ward comprises North Center, Lincoln Square, and the Ravenswood neighborhood in Chicago, and Dara described her community as middle-income, hardworking people who are "house proud." People in this ward sweep the alleys and the sidewalks, and everyone owns a push broom. Everyone. When she moved to her first home in the ward, she found a push broom that the previous owners had left. She wondered why they had left it. She soon learned when she saw everyone on the block sweeping. She has lived in this area for thirty years.

During the many years she has lived in the ward, she never saw a rat. That changed when warmer winters occurred in Chicago and when various construction projects disturbed the rats' homes. She kept getting calls about rats, so she went online to see if there were any other options for her constituents. She learned that Los Angeles, Disneyland, Disneyworld, Rome, and Boston all had TNR programs and that these programs were used to manage rodent issues. She went to Alderman Pawar with this idea, and he was interested enough to have Tree House give a presentation about the program. And then he decided to give it a try.

THE 47TH WARD TRIES CATS AT WORK

About two years after the ward began to use the Cats at Work program, Dara says she has six to eight feral cat colonies (about twenty-five cats) in a ward that covers an area of about three and half miles. She says that, when people call about rats, one of the options that the ward offers is Cats at Work. They have received only one complaint about the program. In general, the colony caretakers and neighbors have been pleased with the program overall. Many of the neighbors regard the cats as their four-legged neighbors who are cleaning up the neighborhood. The caretakers vary from elderly women to young men, and Dara said that caretakers get a lot from the experience. One caretaker has children, and Dara explained that caring for these animals has taught the kids a lot about taking care of other creatures and about being responsible.

The impressive thing about the program is that it's free. Dara's colleague, Jim Poole, estimates that the city of Chicago spends several million dollars a year on staff salaries and poison to deal with the rat problem in Chicago. Jim knew a lot about rats and told me, "Total extermination of rats will never occur. It's a problem that can be managed but never solved."

A BUSY OFFICE

While I was visiting Dara, I gained a new respect for what an alderman's office does on a regular basis. Dara took several phone calls from people who had different needs. One person called about snow removal, and Dara told me that the office has a program for people who are elderly or handicapped. If you're unable to shovel your sidewalk, they will find someone to do it. The ward also has a food pantry, and Dara has started a pet food pantry for those with pets who cannot afford to feed them. In addition, a newsletter is published quarterly by a new nonprofit in the neighborhood—Forward Chicago, which was spun off of the 47th Ward Senior Council. Its mission is to offer people ways to remain active, engaged, and influential, especially as they age in the neighborhood.

As I left Dara's office, we came back to the topic of cats, and she said, "Cats at Work is just one of the various programs that make life better for the people in our ward. It's the humane thing to do. You feel so good when you help the cats. And we need to take responsibility for what we can take responsibility for. We're all connected. We are all part of the solution."

I was inspired.

CHAPTER 24

Sylvester and Tweety: Can't We Just All Get Along?

WHEN I FIRST STARTED REACHING out to other colony caretakers, some of them refused to speak to me. I was dumbfounded. Why wouldn't they speak to me? I've already discussed one of the reasons—the desire to protect the cats through secrecy. The other reason had to do with birds. Yes, birds. The truth is that I'm a bird person. I've saved birds downtown for many years with the Chicago Bird Collision Monitors. Birds fly into the buildings during migration season, and I'm one of the volunteers who patrol areas downtown and save them after they hit the buildings. We have saved thousands of birds. I did this activity for several years, and I still go out to save a bird if I'm in an area and someone is needed to rescue it.

When I asked to speak to some caretakers, one of them investigated my background and found out that I save birds, which made him highly suspicious, and he alerted other caretakers about my proclivities. He and another caretaker refused to speak to me as a result. For some people, you can only love birds or you can only love cats. I love both. The antipathy between some of the cat and bird people is unbelievable. Just mention the topic to individuals who have a point of view, and you can watch an emotional explosion occur right in front of you. Some of the bird lovers believe that cats are the major cause for the decline in birds. Given this charge, I absolutely had to investigate this issue.

One of the sources of the recent uproar is a Smithsonian article by three researchers who estimate that cats kill approximately 1.4 to 3.7 billion birds every year in the United States (Loss, Will, and Marra 2013). This article is often quoted in newspaper articles and in magazines. There are numerous critics of this research, notably Peter Wolf, an analyst at Best Friends Animal Society. Wolf points to several major issues with some of the studies used and the assumptions that were made in creating this estimation (Wolf 2013).

CATS KILL HOW MANY BIRDS?

The first issue that Peter Wolf mentions is that the total number of birds that cats are estimated to kill appears to be implausible (Wolf 2013). The current number of birds who reside in North America and in the United States is currently estimated by researchers, specifically Partners in Flight Science Committee. Partners in Flight is a cooperative effort that involves partnerships among federal, state, and local government agencies; philanthropic foundations; professional organizations; conservation groups; industry; the academic community; and private individuals. Its estimates of the total number of birds are based on data collected by thousands of volunteers who count the number of birds and nests within areas, as well as numbers provided by scientists who study individual species.

Partners in Flight estimates that the total number of birds in the United States is 3.2 billion and in North America, 5.8 billion (Partners in Flight 2013). The Smithsonian article (2013) estimated that cats are killing 1.4 to 3.7 billion birds annually in the United States. If cats were killing this many birds, they would be killing 43 to 100 percent of the US birds each year. If that situation were an actuality, the bird population would be entirely wiped out within one to two years. Even if you take the population estimate for all of North America (5.8 billion birds), 1.4 to 1.7 billion is 24 to 63 percent of birds, which again appears to be an impossibility. If cats had been killing over half of the birds, birds would have been extinct by now.

Interestingly, when this data was compiled in 2004, the estimated number of birds in North America was approximately 4.7 billion birds. When I downloaded this data from 2013, the estimated number of birds in North America was 5.8 billion birds, which suggests that the overall number of birds is increasing, not decreasing. However, some bird species are clearly declining, and the question is why. Some scientists believe that the major causes of declining bird populations are due to humans—habitat loss, climate change, wind turbines, collisions with windows, collisions with automobiles, and pesticides. In my work saving birds downtown, it was seagulls and crows who were a greater menace to the migratory birds than any cats. After the birds hit the windows and were on the ground, it was crows and seagulls that were killing them. I spent more time running to birds in peril from other birds than from cats.

Wolf says assumptions used to create the model estimating the high number of birds killed by cats is another issue that makes the Smithsonian article less than reliable (Wolf 2013). These problematic assumptions include (1) that all household cats go outdoors 100 percent of the time (a finding that is contradicted by research conducted by my own research team, which will be discussed later in this book), (2) a correction factor for the number of prey returned to owners (inflated by a factor of ten to twenty, and (3) assumptions about the number of birds killed by free-roaming cats, which is based largely on small, out-of-date studies.

The research evidence shows that cats kill mammals (for example, rats and mice) more than they do birds (Crooks and Soulé 1999, Kays and DeWan 2004, Mitchell and Beck 1992). The question is, how many birds and which ones? Cats tend to prey on animals that are weaker and sicker because they are easier to catch (Baker et al. 2008, Moller and Erritzoe 2000). These scientific findings have led the Royal Society for the Protection of Birds to declare on its Web site, "Despite the large numbers of birds killed, there is no scientific evidence that predation by cats in gardens is having any impact on bird populations UK-wide. This may be surprising, but many millions of birds die naturally every year, mainly through starvation, disease, or other forms of predation. There is evidence that cats tend to take weak or sickly birds" (RSPB 2014).

There is certainly documented evidence that cats are killing birds in very specific locations. Bird conservationists often point to studies that show the impact of cats on islands off the coast of Australia, New Zealand, and other areas of the Pacific (Global Invasive Species Database 2010). However, it is extremely unwise to extrapolate findings from an island ecosystem or from one specific location to the rest of the world.

CATS ARE A HEALTH HAZARD?

One of the other criticisms leveled at outdoor cats is that they are a health hazard and are a great risk for rabies. The data from the Centers for Disease Control and Prevention from 1995 to 2011 reveal forty-nine documented cases of rabies in humans. Thirty-five of these cases were linked to bats, eleven to dogs (these cases occurred in countries other than the United States), and the remainder listed causes unknown or a fox or raccoon. None were linked to cats (CDC 2014a). A further exploration of the CDC data shows that, in 2010, there were two cases of human rabies and 6,690 cases of rabies in animals. The vast majority of these animals were raccoons (37 percent), skunks (24 percent), and bats (23 percent). The rest were foxes (7 percent), cats (5 percent), cattle (1 percent) and dogs (1 percent). Thus, cats do not appear to be a significant threat when it comes to rabies.

There are some other diseases associated with cats; one is cat scratch disease, which is a bacterial infection that can occur if a cat scratches you. And there are a few other bacterial diseases that cats can carry, such as salmonella, and parasitic diseases, such as toxoplasmosis, tapeworm, and hookworm, which are transmitted through touching cat feces. For those of us who don't touch cat stool directly, there is almost no risk. According to the CDC Web site, you are more likely to get toxoplasmosis from gardening or eating undercooked meat than to get it from cats (CDC 2014b). The only major disease that cats can carry and easily transmit to humans is ringworm, which is a fungal infection. That disease can be transmitted by touching a cat who is infected. My cat, Duke, was diagnosed with ringworm, but neither I nor the other cats were ever infected with it.

I believe the more serious issue is the diseases associated with rodents, who can easily infect humans and other animals. One of these diseases is leptospirosis, a bacterial infection spread through rat urine, which can get into water or soil and can survive for *weeks to months*. Animals and humans can get infected with leptospirosis through contact with this contaminated urine, water, or soil. This bacteria can enter the body through skin or mucous membranes (eyes, nose, or mouth), especially if the skin is broken from a cut or scratch. This disease is apparently on the rise. Outdoor cats could have a significant role in reducing this and other diseases if they're used for rodent control.

TNR DOESN'T WORK?

The last major criticism is that TNR programs don't reduce the number of feral cats. The evidence presented to Cook County in 2013 shows that these program do work, but it's unwise to extrapolate findings from one area of the country to the entire United States. The organization that has collected the most data on the effects of TNR programs is Alley Cat Allies, which has documented the impact of TNR programs all over the world.

One of the advantages of TNR programs is that caretakers can track the number of cats in a colony because they feed them every day. They can easily see if the number of cats is increasing, decreasing, or staying the same. And when numerous cities track the number of colony cats across many areas, a pattern starts to emerge. One of the notable large-scale TNR programs is in Rome, where approximately eight thousand cats were neutered and then returned to their colony locations over a nine-year period (1991 to 2000). Over the course of this time period, 103 colonies were followed. The researchers found that the size of colonies consistently decreased by about 16 percent in three years and by about 32 percent over 6 years (Natoli et al. 2006). Similar results have been shown in South Africa, where researchers found that neutering just over half of the cats in a colony led to a stabilization of the number of colony cat members (Jones and Downs 2011).

Studies in the United States have shown similar results. Researchers at the University of Central Florida conducted an eleven-year study on a TNR program. They found that the number of cats born on campus during that time declined by 66 percent and that 83 percent of the cats had been colony members for more than six years (Levy, Gale, and Gale 2003). Texas A&M University also followed the TNR cats on their campus and discovered that the colonies' numbers were greatly reduced after only one year (Hughes and Slater 2002). Similar results have been observed in North Carolina (Stoskopf and Nutter 2004), San Francisco (Morrissey 2013), and Atlantic City (Alley Cat Allies 2014a). And my favorite example comes from the Adams Morgan neighborhood in DC, which was the impetus for the creation of Alley Cat Allies by Becky Robinson. In 1990, Becky and her cofounder, Louise Holton, found fifty-four cats, whom they trapped and neutered. Most of them were returned to the area. Today, there are currently no cats living in that alley. The last member of that colony died in 2007 at the age of seventeen (Alley Cat Allies 2014).

TRAP AND EUTHANIZE (T&E) IS NOT THE SOLUTION

One of the solutions offered for dealing with feral cats is euthanasia—trapping and killing them. The reason that approach doesn't work is because of the vacuum effect. Cats live near food and shelter sources. When cats are trapped and euthanized, other cats move into that area and begin to live there. All that trapping and euthanizing does is to create a vicious cycle, especially given the reproductive capabilities of cats.

The vacuum effect has been documented among many species, including possums (Ji et al. 2001) and badgers (Killian et al 2007). And it has been demonstrated over and over again with feral cats. One example occurred in Newburyport, Massachusetts, in 1990. Approximately three hundred stray and feral cats lived along the Merrimack River, and the city brought in a company to trap and kill the cats. Although 10 percent of the cats were killed, within two years, those cats had been replaced by others who had moved into the area. In 1992, the Merrimack River Feline Rescue Society began a TNR program, which stabilized and reduced the colony (*LA Times* 2009). Today there are no colony cats living in that area. The last member of that colony died in 2009 at the age of sixteen (Alley Cat Allies 2014).

One question I have is why colonies are able to get smaller and disappear over time given this vacuum effect. I believe that cats' natural territoriality leads them to fend off other cats throughout their lifetime, which is why additional cats don't move into an area that supports fewer colony cats over time.

Animal control organizations are highly familiar with the vacuum effect and have turned to TNR as a more effective method for dealing with feral cats. They simply found that trapping and euthanizing cats wasn't working. An example of this change in opinion occurred with the Maricopa County Animal Care and Control executives, who explained, "We have over 20 years of documented proof that traditional ways of dealing with feral cats don't work. The catch and kill method of population control (trap a cat, bring it to a shelter, ask that the cat be euthanized) has not reduced the number of feral cats. The cat may be gone, but now there is room for another cat to move in … So, catch and kill actually makes the problem worse" (Alley Cat Allies 2014b). Similar points of view can be found among other animal control and animal advocacy organizations, including the National Animal Control Association, the American Society for the Prevention of Cruelty to Animals (ASPCA 2014), and other humane societies around the United States (Alley Cat Allies 2014b).

WHAT IS THE SOLUTION?

Clearly, the solution is not trapping and euthanizing feral cats, given that this activity perpetuates a vicious cycle. Some people have suggested taking all the feral cats, trapping them, and then locating them in a building. As I learned from research we conducted, the results of which appear in the next chapter, that solution is untenable, given the current number of feral and stray cats who live outdoors.

TNR is clearly the solution for stabilizing and eventually reducing the feral cat population. However, feral cats do prey upon birds and other animals and should be located in areas that make sense. Feral cats should not be located near bird sanctuaries or near public parks where there is a large amount of bird traffic. And when there are too many cats in an area, some of them should be relocated. TNR is clearly the solution, but it needs to be enacted wisely. And caretakers need to ensure that community cats are not a nuisance to neighbors and that they provide a real service.

CHAPTER 25

Predominant Attitudes in the United States about Stray Cats, TNR, and Spaying or Neutering

SO HOW MANY CATS ARE actually living in the United States? And what are the predominant attitudes about cats, TNR, and spaying or neutering? Given that TNR offers a solution for feral cats, I was curious how most Americans think about these issues. I couldn't find the kind of information I wanted, so I decided to conduct a research study on these issues.

By way of background, I own a market research firm that does complicated strategic market research studies for Fortune 500 companies. We help major corporations answer major business questions, such as whether they should acquire another company, what products to launch, which advertising they should use, what segments they should target in a market, and what the size of a market is for a potential product. We conduct qualitative and quantitative research, such as focus groups, in-depth interviews, and surveys to help companies make major strategic decisions (Beall 2010).

My firm, Beall Research, created an Internet survey that covered attitudes toward cats, TNR, and spaying and neutering and was answered by a representative sample of 1,500[1] people in the United States. We weighted this data so that it represents the US population in terms of age, gender, Hispanic origin, and race. Thus, the final data represents what Americans think and feel about these issues.

NUMBER OF CATS AND CAT OWNERSHIP

We first asked all respondents to indicate how many cats live in their household and stay inside all the time, how many live indoors and go outside, how many household cats live outdoors 100 percent of the time, and then how many stray or feral cats are on their property and whether they feed them. We gave them the following definition so they would understand the term feral cat.

For the purposes of this survey, *feral cats* are cats that are born in the wild. They are different from *stray cats*, which are pet cats that have been lost or abandoned and were not born in the wild. The two types of cats look the same.

Thus, each respondent provided information on the following:

- » Number of cats in their household who live inside 100 percent of the time
- » Number of cats in their household who live indoors but go outside
- » Number of cats in their household who live outside 100 percent of the time and whom they feed, who *are not stray or feral cats*
- » Number of stray or feral cats on their property whom they do not feed
- » Number of stray or feral cats on their property whom they feed regularly

---

1   Provides a confidence interval of ±2.5 percent at the 95 percent confidence level.

Because each respondent represented a US household, the number of cats in each category was then multiplied by the total number of households in the United States (121,122,161 as of 2013). We found that there are approximately 184 million cats in the United States. Approximately 37 percent of US households have a cat, with an average number of 2.1 cats. Thus, there are about 95 million cats in US households. About 62 percent of cats are completely indoor cats and the remainder (38 percent) go outside some of the time. There are also an additional 20.5 million cats who are part of the household and who live outdoors all the time.

In terms of stray and feral cats, we learned that there are approximately 69 million stray or feral cats; 28 million of them are fed and 41 million are not. If you include the pet cats who live outdoors 100 percent of the time, there are approximately 89 million cats who live completely outdoors. Thus, 48 percent of all US cats live outdoors. Below is a pie chart that shows the number of cats.

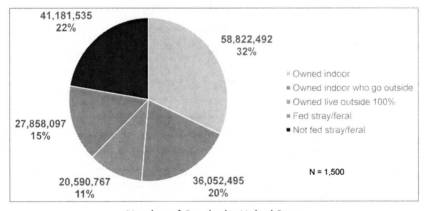

41,181,535
22%

58,822,492
32%

27,858,097
15%

20,590,767
11%

36,052,495
20%

⬚ Owned indoor
■ Owned indoor who go outside
⬚ Owned live outside 100%
⬚ Fed stray/feral
■ Not fed stray/feral

N = 1,500

Number of Cats in the United States

If anyone was feeding cats who lived outdoors, we asked them if they had a feral cat colony that they regularly feed. We provided the following definition: *A feral cat colony is a group of feral cats that lives in a single place for a sustained period of time.* If they said they had a feral cat colony, we asked how many cats were in the colony.

We learned that 6 percent of respondents currently have a feral cat colony with an average of four cats, which means that there are 7.8 million colonies with a total of about 32 million cats.

Percentage who have a feral cat colony (n = 1500)	6%
Average number of cats per colony (n = 97)	4.1
Estimated total number of feral cat colonies in U.S.	7,832,566
Estimated total number of cats in feral cat colonies in the U.S.	31,956,871

Feral Colony Caretakers

We were interested in learning more about who the colony caretakers are, so we looked at their gender, age, household income, and whether or not they were cat owners. We found that current caretakers are slightly more likely to be female, more likely to be twenty-five to thirty-nine years of age, and very likely to have cats as pets. They range in terms of their household income. This data is shown below.

	Current Colony Caretakers (N = 97)
Male	43%
Female	57%
18-24 years old	14%
25-39 years old	44%
40-59 years old	29%
60+ years old	12%
Cat owners	75%
Less than $35,000 in household income	27%
$35,000 – $49,999 in household income	12%
$50,000 - $74,999 in household income	21%
$75,000 - $99,999 in household income	22%
$100,000+ in household income	18%

Demographics of Current Colony Caretakers

We asked Americans where they acquired their pet cat and almost a third (29 percent) got them from the outside—it was a stray, which is another indication of how many cats live outdoors. Another 28 percent got them from a family or friend, and a quarter (24 percent) got them from a pet shelter. Getting cats from pet stores, cattery/breeders, or some other way is less common. See this data below.

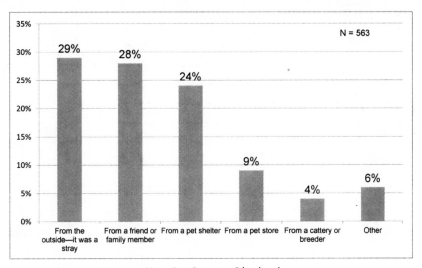

How Pet Cat was Obtained

ATTITUDES TOWARD STRAY CATS

When we asked how people felt about stray cats, we found that Americans are not against them. The predominant attitude toward stray cats is one of pity and a desire to help. About half (51 percent) of those in this survey said they feel sorry for stray cats and about one-third (37 percent) said they wish they could help them. About one-quarter (27 percent) try to help stray cats when it's possible. The table on the next page shows the responses that people have to stray cats. Note that you could select more than one response when answering this question.

Which of the following best describes your feelings about stray cats?

N = 1,500	Percentage
I feel sorry for them	51%
I wish I could help them	37%
I don't mind them	30%
I try to help them when I can	27%
I don't have any feelings about stray cats	12%
I consider them to be pests	10%
I consider them to be dangerous	8%
I hate all cats	6%
I hate stray cats	5%
I am afraid of them	4%
Other (please specify)	3%

Predominant Feelings about Stray Cats

We were curious about people who hate stray cats (or all cats), which appears to be about 5 to 6 percent of the US population, so we asked about the reasons for their hatred. The major reasons are that cats are perceived as a nuisance, they shed hair, and the person has been scratched in the past. Interestingly, almost two in ten people perceive cats as too aloof or "snobby," which suggests that they don't like cats because they perceive cats as unfriendly or uninterested in them. The table below shows the major reasons why people hate cats.

What are the major reasons you hate cats?

N = 142	Percentage
Cats are a nuisance	35%
Cats shed hair everywhere	27%
I have been scratched by cats in the past	24%
Cats are snobby	18%
Cats are aloof and too independent	18%
Cats carry diseases	15%
My family has always hated cats	15%
I have been bitten by cats in the past	10%

N = 142	Percentage
Cats bother my dogs	10%
I have allergies to cats	8%
I am fearful of cats	8%
Cats don't like me	6%
Cats kill birds	4%
I don't like animals	4%
Other (please specify)	6%

Major Reasons Why Cats are Hated

We were curious whether people feel that leaving stray cats where they are is a good idea, so we asked the following question: *If you saw a stray cat in your community and could only choose between two courses of action—leaving the cat where it is outside or having the cat caught and then put down—which would you consider to be the more humane option for the cat?* The vast majority of people (73 percent) said that they would leave the cat where it is. This data is consistent with previous data collected by Alley Cat Allies in 2007.

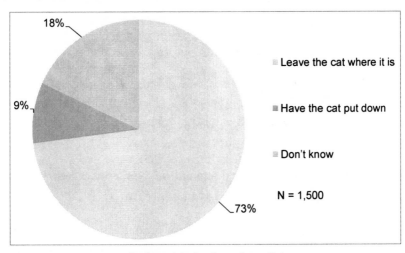

Preferred Action for a Stray Cat

We then asked the same question but said that the cat would die in two years from being hit by a car. Half of respondents wanted to leave the cat where it was and one-quarter were unsure what to do. This data is also consistent with that from a previous study conducted by Alley Cat Allies.

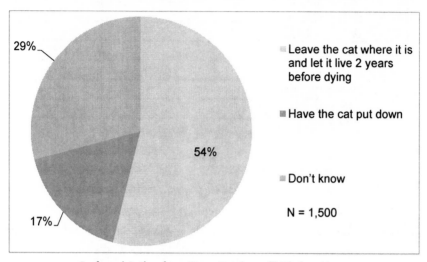

Preferred Action for a Stray Cat that will Die in 2 Years

In order to understand the predominant attitudes about euthanasia, we also asked how people feel about putting cats down in pet shelters. We asked them to select one of the following statements:

» I believe that shelters should put down cats when there are too many of them.

» I believe that shelters should only put down cats that are either too ill or too aggressive to be adopted.

» Other.

The large majority believe that shelters should only put cats down when they are too ill or too aggressive to be adopted.

Thus, the majority of Americans feel sorry for stray cats, would like to help them, and do not believe that euthanizing them is the answer, even if they know they will have a shortened life. And the majority of Americans do not believe that pet shelters should put cats down because of overpopulation.

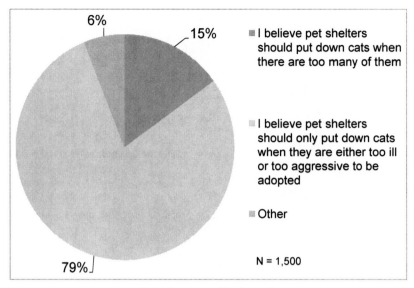

Attitudes toward Euthanasia

ATTITUDES TOWARD TNR PROGRAMS

We shared a description of TNR programs and asked if Americans were familiar with this program. Below is the description:

Some of the cats you see outside are *feral cats*. Feral cats are cats that are born in the wild. They are different from *stray cats*, which are pet cats that have been lost or abandoned and were not born in the wild. The two types of cats do not look different.

There is a simple program to help feral cats. It's called the Trap-Neuter-Return (TNR) program. With TNR programs, feral cats are humanely trapped and then spayed/neutered so they can't have kittens. After they have recovered from surgery, they are relocated or returned to their original location.

This program stabilizes and reduces feral cat populations and improves the cats' lives. The behaviors associated with mating, such as yowling, spraying, and fighting stop after cats are spayed/neutered.

The majority of Americans had not heard about this program or knew very little about it. Almost three-quarters (71 percent) had never even heard of TNR. And only 5 percent of the respondent had heard of TNR programs and were very familiar with them.

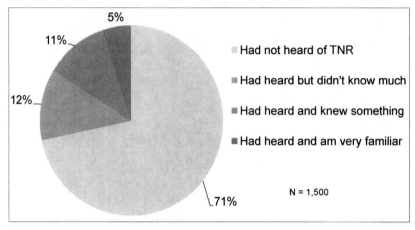

Awareness of TNR

We then asked how positively or negatively respondents felt about TNR programs, given the description we provided, and to indicate using a 10-point scale where a 1 indicated they felt "extremely negative" about TNR programs and a 10 indicated they felt "extremely positive" about them. The majority of respondents were extremely positive about TNR, and just over half (55 percent) gave the program a rating of 8, 9, or 10 (see figure below).

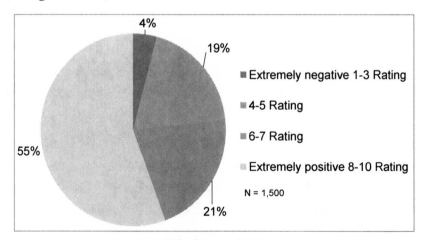

Attitude toward TNR

If you divide the respondents into two groups—those who are extremely positive toward TNR and those who are less positive about it, it becomes clear that women, households that are not at the poverty level, cat owners, and people who feel sorry for stray cats and wish they could help them are most positive about TNR. The table below shows this data.

	Passive Acceptors or Detractors of TNR (1-7 Rating) N = 679 a	Supporters of TNR (8, 9, 10 rating) N = 821 b
Male	52% (b)	41%
Female	48%	59% (a)
Less than $35K in household income	34% (b)	26%
$35K+ in household income	66%	72% (a)
Cat owner	25%	48% (a)
Predominant feelings about stray cats		
I feel sorry for them	38%	61% (a)
I wish I could help them	25%	47% (a)
I try to help them when I can	17%	35% (a)

Differences between Supporters and Detractors/Passive Supporters of TNR

We then provided some additional information about TNR programs and asked people how important this information is to them. They indicated importance using a 10-point scale where a 1 indicated the information was "not at all important" and a 10 indicated it was "extremely important" to them. The information we provided falls into the following categories:

REDUCTION/STABILIZATION OF FERAL CAT COLONIES

» TNR programs have been shown to stabilize and reduce the feral cat population

Public Health/Diseases

» Cats in TNR programs are monitored for diseases and have not been shown to be a health hazard

» Cats in TNR programs are regularly vaccinated and are not at risk to transmit rabies or other feline disease to other cats

Rodent control

» Cats who are part of TNR programs have been successfully used to get rid of rats and mice

» Cats in TNR programs live in urban, suburban, and rural areas and have been effective at reducing the number of rats in those areas

Cat Health

» Cats in TNR programs are shown to live as long as cats who live indoors

» Cats in TNR programs are less likely to fight (because they have been spayed or neutered) and are less likely to be injured by other cats

» Cats in TNR programs belong in a colony where they are regularly fed by a colony caretaker and therefore do not have to hunt for their food

» Cats in TNR programs are fed by a caretaker and are similar in weight and size to indoor cats

Local Humane Societies

» Local humane societies monitor feral cat colonies and ensure they are being properly cared for

» Local humane societies are generally the ones who trap, neuter, and return or relocate the cats

Bird Outcomes

» Cats in TNR programs have not been shown to significantly reduce bird populations

After rating the importance of each item, respondents indicated which information was *most* important to them. As you can see from the table below, many items are extremely important to Americans. The most important items concern the fact that the cats in TNR programs are regularly vaccinated and do not transmit diseases and that these programs stabilize and reduce feral cat populations.

N = 1,500 Scale is 1-10 with 1 = Not at all important, 10 = Extremely important	% Who Gave Top 2 Box Importance Rating (9-10)	% Who Identified Information as <u>Most</u> Important
Cats in TNR programs are regularly vaccinated and are not at risk to transmit rabies, or other feline diseases to other cats.	53%	17%
TNR programs have been shown to stabilize and reduce the feral-cat populations	49%	15%
Cats in TNR programs are monitored for diseases and have not been shown to be a health hazard	49%	11%
Cats in TNR programs are less likely to fight (because they have been spayed/neutered) and they are less likely to be injured by other cats	45%	3%
Cats who are part of TNR programs have been successfully used to get rid of rats and mice	45%	9%
Local humane societies monitor feral cat colonies and ensure they are being properly cared for	44%	11%
Cats in TNR programs live in urban, suburban and rural areas and have been effective at reducing the number of rats in those areas	44%	8%
Local humane societies are generally the ones who trap, neuter and return/relocate the cats	41%	6%
Cats in TNR programs are shown to live as long as cats who are indoors	39%	6%
Cats in TNR programs belong in a colony where they are regularly fed by a colony caretaker and therefore do not have to hunt for their food	38%	8%
Cats in TNR programs are fed by a caretaker and are similar in size and weight to indoor cats	37%	3%
Cats in TNR programs have not been shown to significantly reduce bird populations	31%	2%

Importance of Information about TNR

If you combine the items that are related, you can see the following patterns. Most people regard public health, cat health, and the fact that humane societies are involved with feral cat colonies as the most important information about TNR programs (see the table below).

N = 1,500	Percentage Who Identified Information as **Most Important**
Public Health/Disease Control	28%
• Cats in TNR programs are monitored for diseases and have not been shown to be a health hazard	
• Cats in TNR programs are regularly vaccinated and are not at risk to transmit rabies, or other feline diseases to other cats.	
Cat Health	20%
• Cats in TNR programs are shown to live as long as cats who are indoors	
• Cats in TNR programs are fed by a caretaker and are similar in size and weight to indoor cats	
• Cats in TNR programs belong in a colony where they are regularly fed by a colony caretaker and therefore do not have to hunt for their food	
• Cats in TNR programs are less likely to fight (because they have been spayed/neutered) and they are less likely to be injured by other cats	
Local Humane Societies	19%
• Local humane societies monitor feral cat colonies and ensure they are being properly cared for	
• Local humane societies are generally the ones who trap, neuter and return/relocate the cats	
Rodent Control	16%
• Cats who are part of TNR programs have been successfully used to get rid of rats and mice	
• Cats in TNR programs live in urban, suburban and rural areas and have been effective at reducing the number of rats in those areas	
Stabilization/Reduction Feral Cat Population	15%
• TNR programs have been shown to stabilize and reduce the feral-cat populations	
Effects on Birds	2%
• Cats in TNR programs have not been shown to significantly reduce bird populations	

Importance of Aggregated Information about TNR

After respondents indicated which information was most important to them, we asked what impact this information had on their feelings about TNR programs. They used a 10-point scale where a 1 indicated that they felt much more negatively and a 10 indicated they felt much more positively about TNR programs after learning this information. As the figure below shows, the information that was important to them made about two-thirds (64 percent) of respondents feel much more positively about TNR.

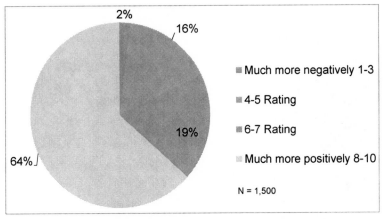

Impact of Most Important Information on Attitude toward TNR

We then asked how likely they would be to support a TNR program in their area. However we indicated that we were not indicating financial support. As shown in the figure below, over half (58 percent) of Americans would be extremely likely to support a TNR program.

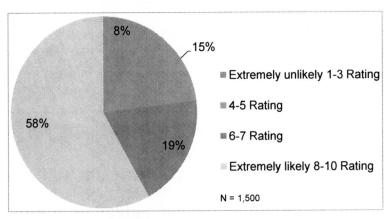

Likelihood to Support a TNR Program

We then asked respondents the following question: "If there were a Trap-Neuter-Return program in your area, *how likely would you be to become a colony caretaker* if you knew it involved feeding feral cats twice a day and monitoring their health?" (We didn't ask this question of current colony caretakers.) We found that 20 percent of Americans said they would be highly likely to become caretakers (they gave an 8, 9, or 10 likelihood rating to this question). The data is shown below in the figure below.

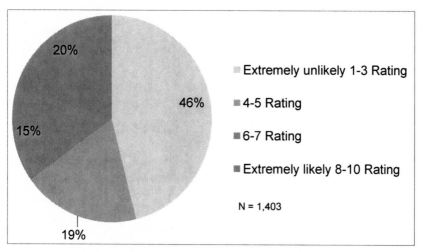

Likelihood to Become a Colony Caretaker

Using this data, we estimated that, if more people learned about TNR, there would be an additional 9 million colony caretakers, which would yield a total of 17 million colonies (see the table below).

Current estimated number of feral cat colonies in the United States	7,832,566
Estimated percentage of potential colony caretakers	7.7%
Estimated number of potential feral cat colonies	9,326,406
Estimated TOTAL number of feral cat colonies (including actual and potential colonies)	17,158,972

Actual and Potential Colony Caretakers in U.S.

ATTITUDES TOWARD SPAYING OR NEUTERING CATS

We were also interested in how Americans view spaying and neutering, so we asked whether the cat who lives in their home is spayed or neutered and explained that meant the cat had been "fixed" and could not have kittens. About 82 percent of the cats in the household had been spayed or neutered. We then asked how important it is to spay or neuter cats so they can't reproduce, and almost three-quarters of respondents said it's extremely important (see the figure below).

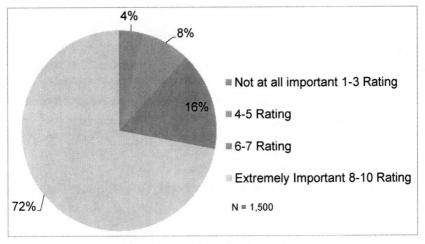

Importance of Spaying/Neutering

We then provided some information about spaying and neutering. Below is what we shared:

Cat Euthanasia

» There is already an overpopulation of cats in the United States, and over 1.5 million cats are put down every year

» There are very few no-kill shelters in the United States, and the animal shelters put down 70 percent of cats and kittens brought to them each year

» The vast majority of kittens who are under five weeks of age are put down at shelters because they are not weaned and require bottle feeding every few hours

» The majority of kittens and cats taken to shelters are never adopted

Cat Behaviors

> » Cats who are not spayed or neutered are more likely to fight with other cats

> » Cats who are not spayed or neutered are more likely to spray their urine inside and outside

> » Cats who are not spayed or neutered are more likely to howl at night

> » Indoor cats will not display many annoying mating behaviors (for example, howling, spraying, pleading to go out) if they are spayed or neutered

Cat Health

> » Cats who have been spayed or neutered live longer than those who have not

> » There are veterinarians who offer low cost or no-cost spays or neutering

> » There are programs that offer free transportation for spaying or neutering

It Starts Early

> » Kittens begin reproducing at about four to six months of age

We asked people to rate how important this information is to them using a 10-point scale where a 1 meant it was "not at all important" and a 10 meant it was "extremely important." After they rated the importance of each item, they indicated which information was most important to them. As you can see from the table on the next page, respondents reported that the most important information is that there are 1.5 million cats euthanized every year, which is about 70 percent of the cats in shelters, and that there are veterinarians who offer low cost or no-cost spaying or neutering.

N = 1,500 Scale is 1-10 with 1 = Not at all important, 10 = Extremely important	% Who Gave Top 2 Box Importance Rating (9-10)	% Who Identified Information as <u>Most</u> Important
There is already an overpopulation of cats in the U.S. and over 1.5 million cats are put down every year	50%	20%
There are veterinarians who offer low cost or no-cost spaying/neutering	46%	18%
There are very few no-kill shelters in the U.S. and the animal shelters put down 70% of cats and kittens brought to them each year	44%	14%
Cats who have been spayed/neutered live longer than those who have not	44%	7%
The majority of kittens and cats taken to shelters are never adopted	43%	7%
Indoor cats will not display many annoying mating behaviors (e.g., howling, spraying, pleading to go out) if they are spayed/neutered	42%	7%
The vast majority of kittens who are under 5 weeks of age are generally put down at shelters because they are not weaned and require bottle feeding every few hours	41%	7%
There are programs that offer free transportation for spaying/neutering	39%	7%
Kittens begin reproducing at about 4-6 months of age	39%	5%
Cats who are not spayed/neutered are more likely to spray their urine inside and outside	38%	5%
Cats who are not spayed/neutered are more likely to fight with other cats	36%	3%
Cats who are not spayed/neutered are more likely to howl at night	33%	2%

Importance of Information about Spaying/Neutering

If you combine these items into categories, you see the following results in the table on the next page. Clearly the information that so many cats are being euthanized and the fact that there are programs to assist people with spaying or neutering is most important.

N = 1,500	Percentage Who Identified Information as **Most** Important
Cat Euthanasia	48%
• There is already an overpopulation of cats in the U.S. and over 1.5 million cats are put down every year	
• There are very few no-kill shelters in the U.S. and the animal shelters put down 70% of cats and kittens brought to them each year	
• The vast majority of kittens who are under 5 weeks of age are generally put down at shelters because they are not weaned and require bottle feeding every few hours	
• The majority of kittens and cats taken to shelters are never adopted	
Programs to help	35%
• There are veterinarians who offer low cost or no-cost spays/neutering	
• There are programs that offer free transportation for spaying/neutering	
Cat Behaviors	17%
• Cats who are not spayed/neutered are more likely to fight with other cats	
• Cats who are not spayed/neutered are more likely to spray their urine inside and outside	
• Cats who are not spayed/neutered are more likely to howl at night	
• Indoor cats will not display many annoying mating behaviors (e.g., howling, spraying, pleading to go out) if they are spayed/neutered	
Cat Health	7%
• Cats who have been spayed/neutered live longer than those who have not	
It starts early	5%
• Kittens begin reproducing at about 4-6 months of age	

Importance of Amalgamated Information about Spaying/Neutering

We then inquired how the most important information made them feel about spaying or neutering cats. About 70 percent indicated they felt much more positively about fixing their cat after learning this information. This data is shown in the next figure.

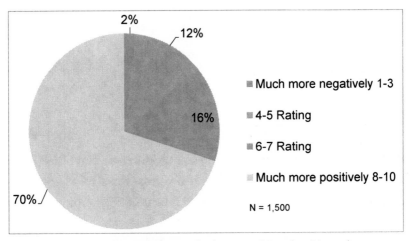

Impact of Information on Attitudes toward Spaying/Neutering

We then asked how likely people who had an intact cat (not spayed or neutered) would be to spay or neuter their cat after learning this information. We learned that almost two-thirds (61 percent) of those with a cat that hadn't been fixed said they were extremely likely to do so given this information (see figure below).

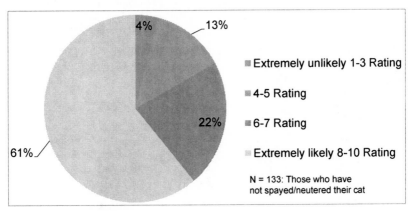

Likelihood to Spay/Neuter after Learning Information

RATS AND BIRDS

Given the controversy surrounding the number of birds killed, we asked all respondents about whether a cat from their household or whether a stray or feral cat on their property does any of the following:

- » Kills rats

- » Kills mice

- » Kills birds

- » Kills rabbits

- » Kills other animals

All data for cats who live indoors and go outdoors was combined, and all data for cats that live outdoors (in other words, stray, feral, and owned cats who live outdoors 100 percent of the time) was combined.

As you can see in the figure below, we found that about 20 percent of indoor cats who go outside and 28 percent of outdoor cats kill rats. Approximately 40 to 47 percent of households have a cat (indoors or outdoors) that kills mice, and about one-third (32 to 33 percent) have an indoor or outdoor cat (including stray or feral cats) that kills birds. About 10 to 11 percent of American homes have a cat inside or outside that kills rabbits.

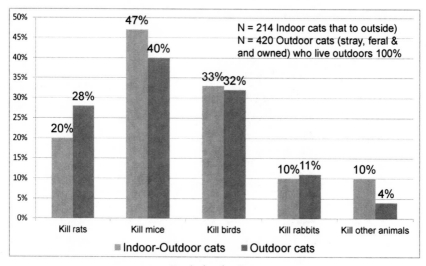

Predation by Cats

We estimated the number of rats and birds that are being killed by using the following numbers:

- » Total household in the United States

» The number of households that have an indoor cat that goes outside and kills birds or rats

» The number of households in the United States that have a cat on their property who kills birds or rats but does not live inside the household

» The average number of birds or rats being killed by all indoor cats that go outside

» The average number of birds or rats being killed by all outdoor cats (owned and stray or feral cats)

We found that cats who live indoors and go outside kill approximately 2.5 million rats. Outdoor cats kill about 14.8 million rats. Thus, the total number of rats being killed by cats is about 17.3 million rats. The table below shows the specific numbers we calculated using data from our study.

Number of Households in the United States	121,122,161	
Number of households with indoor cats that go outdoors and kill rats	2.87%	3,472,169
Average number of rats killed by indoor cats that go outdoors for each household in one year	.73	
Total number of rats killed by indoor cats that can go outdoors in one year	2,534,683	
Number of households with outdoor cats (including stray/feral) who kill rats	7.87%	9,528,277
Average number of rats killed by all outdoor cats for each household in one year	1.56	
Total number or rats killed by all outdoor cats in one year	14,864,112	
Total number of rats killed by all cats in one year	**17,398,795**	

Number of Rats Being Killed

In contrast, we found that indoor cats who go outdoors kill about 6.7 million birds. And outdoor cats (owned and stray or feral cats who live outside 100 percent of the time) kill about 14.8 million birds. Thus, the total number of birds killed by cats in an average year as reported by owners and observers of stray or feral cats is about 21.6 million birds. See the table on the next page for the numbers that were used to derive this number. If you want further detail on how these numbers were calculated, this information is located in Appendix B: Calculation Methods.

Number of Households in the United States	121,122,161	
Number of households with indoor cats that go outdoors and kill birds	4.67%	5,652,367
Average number of birds killed by indoor cats that go outdoors for each household in one year	1.2	
Total number of birds killed by indoor cats that can go outdoors in one year	6,782,841	
Number of households with outdoor cats (including stray/feral) who kill birds	8.93%	10,820,246
Average number of birds killed by all outdoor cats for each household in one year	1.37	
Total number or birds killed by all outdoor cats in one year	14,823,737	
Total number of birds killed by all cats in one year	21,606,578	

Number of Birds Killed

The question is how accurate these numbers are, given that the numbers are reported by humans about cats, especially stray and feral cats, who can be fearful of people. In a study conducted by the University of Georgia (Loyd et al. 2013) researchers attached cameras onto fifty-five cats to see how many animals they killed. They found that, on average, cats bring back about a quarter of their prey, 49 percent of prey is left, and the remainder is eaten. If we assume that our estimates are off by a factor of four, the total number of rats and birds killed would be 69,595,178 rats and 86,426,313 birds. Therefore, it is highly unlikely that feral cats are the major reason for a decline in the number of birds.

CHAPTER 26

Becky Robinson and Alley Cat Allies

ONE OF THE NAMES THAT kept coming up was Becky Robinson. People would tell me that I really should talk to Becky Robinson. She's the one who advocated for TNR programs in the United States and her organization, Alley Cat Allies, is the national advocacy group for cats. If you want information about stray and feral cats or want to learn about the research behind TNR, you will undoubtedly come across Alley Cat Allies. So I contacted Becky. These days, Becky is extremely busy, so getting on her calendar is no easy task. A few weeks after I contacted her office, Becky and I talked about what prompted her to become a national advocate for TNR and for cats.

EARLY LIFE

Becky grew up in McPherson, a small town in central Kansas, which has a main street with a few shops and many miles of wheat fields around it. Becky's family had lived in that area since the 1870s, when her ancestor Captain George Robinson first settled there. He had a dugout on the side of a hill—a part of property that is still held in the family today.

Becky grew up in a family that taught her the value of all living creatures. She learned from her father at an early age not to be afraid of spiders, insects, and snakes. He explained to her that we are all part of an ecosystem and that each animal has a role to play in it. She remembers fondly that one of the things she learned from her family was that, if you could help animals, you should. She recalls driving down the roads with her father, and if they saw a turtle trying to get across, they would stop the car and help it cross the road. If there was an injured coyote or bird or raccoon, they would help in any way they could.

She recounted how her family would try to save rattlesnakes before the rattlesnake roundups, which occur in the Midwest. Rattlesnake roundups are somewhat like a community fair. Rattlesnakes are first captured and then wrangled, skinned, and eaten. Hundreds to thousands of rattlesnakes are killed. Animal advocates and environmentalists decry these activities. Becky's family was in agreement. Before each roundup, her father would save several rattlesnakes. He would bring them home and hold them until after the roundup. Her father always loved snakes and lizards, and he explained that the snakes are not active predators of humans and that they have a role in the environment. You have to understand nature, respect it, and protect it, he explained to her.

One of her favorite family activities involved going to watch prairie dogs. Prairie dogs live in burrows under the ground. They live in collections of colonies or very large "towns," which can cover hundreds of acres. Becky and her family would go watch the prairie dogs for hours. But in order to watch them, you had to be very quiet. You had to lie or sit next to their hole and be very still—not move a muscle or make a noise. When the prairie dogs felt safe, they would come out of their homes and eat and play. Becky said those early experiences taught her that you have to work within an animal's world and that you have to be extremely patient. Those lessons would serve her well later in life when she had to trap feral cats.

When Becky was ten years old, her parents divorced and she lived with her father, near her aunt and grandmother. She spent a great deal of time with her aunt and grandmother, strong, independent women who impressed upon her that there are real problems that need to be solved and that it's up to us to solve them. Her aunt had a weekly column in the local newspaper that educated people about how to care for animals. Becky often thought about real-world problems as a teenager, so it wasn't surprising that she went to college and graduate school to become a social worker. Throughout this period, she always rescued stray cats and dogs.

A PERSONAL EXPERIENCE LEADS TO ANIMAL ADVOCACY

One day, Becky found a sweet orange male cat who was a stray and brought him home to her apartment. Her roommate adamantly told her she could not keep the cat. Becky was unsure of what to do, so she drove down to the animal pound. Becky recounted the story almost thirty years later, but she remembers it as if it happened yesterday. The experience was harrowing. She drove into a dark, industrial area with large, gray buildings. She walked into a dirty, old building that looked like an old welding plant. She handed the orange tabby over to the worker and walked out. As she drove away, she had a sickening feeling. Her throat closed up. *What did I do?* she asked herself. She got home and called her aunt and asked her what would become of the cat. Her aunt told her that it was likely the cat would be euthanized. Becky felt sick. She realized at this point that she would need to have the courage to stand up for animals and not hand them over to a pound because a roommate didn't want them. And she had to be around people who could support her ideals. She moved out of her apartment.

She realized after that experience that the system for animal welfare was broken. Taking stray animals to animal pounds wasn't the answer. Those animals weren't being helped; they were being killed. She attended a lecture by a woman named Syndee Brinkman, who told the audience that letters to elected officials make a difference and that one of the major things that people write about is animals. It was the number-two issue that people wrote about.

Becky became involved in the protests for the Silver Spring monkeys, thusly named because they lived in the Institute of Behavioral Research in Silver Spring, Maryland. The monkeys lived in small, filthy cages and were not given veterinary care, despite the fact that they were subjected to debilitating surgeries and had open wounds and other problems. Animal rights protesters inhabited tents and protested the way the monkeys were being treated. Becky was one of them. Police eventually entered the institute and removed the monkeys, charging the researcher with seventeen counts of animal cruelty and failing to provide adequate veterinary care. The people who began this protest founded PETA—People for Ethical Treatment of Animals. Becky realized that individuals can make a huge difference, and she went to work for Syndee Brinkman in DC.

A CHANCE ENCOUNTER IN AN ALLEY

A few years later in 1990, Becky had plans to celebrate her birthday with a friend, Louise Holton. They were supposed to meet at a restaurant in Adams-Morgan, but there was no parking nearby, so Becky parked several blocks away and cut through an alley on her way to the restaurant. As she walked along, she saw numerous feral cats, whom she described as beautiful and healthy. After dinner, she and Louise walked back through the same alley. They both stopped when they saw the cats and agreed that they were going to help them. Then next day, Louise called a shelter, which was uninterested in the issue. Louise was from South Africa, where TNR was practiced, and she believed that these feral cats could be helped with a TNR program. Becky and Louise eventually trapped fifty-four cats, had them spayed or neutered, and returned the unsociable ones to the alley where they were regularly fed by several people. The friendly cats were adopted. Alley Cat Allies (ACA) was born.

The early days for Alley Cat Allies were difficult. Becky and Louise resorted to taking donations from friends to help the feral cats. The biggest issue they encountered was that there were no veterinarians who were willing to spay and neuter the cats. Eventually they convinced a local veterinarian to do the surgeries. Becky said that she and Louise made a lot of mistakes in the process. But they documented everything they were doing so they could provide protocols to other caregivers and grassroots groups around the country. These protocols are now used by veterinarians, animal hospitals, and humane societies all over the United States who practice TNR.

In the beginning, Alley Cat Allies was an advocacy group that educated people about TNR in order to give cats a better life. Animal advocates began spreading the word about Becky and Louise's work, and they began receiving thousands of calls. The demand for their expertise was enormous. One night, Becky came back to her home to eighty voice mail messages—all from people looking for information about or help with feral cats.

ALLEY CAT ALLIES BEGINS TO GROW

Because ACA had very little money, Becky continued to work for other organizations and to work for ACA in her spare time. She regularly spoke at conventions, gave interviews, and educated as many people as she could. She was a tireless and unpaid advocate. In fact, ACA's first employee was neither Becky nor Louise. The organization's founders had so little money that they could not even afford to hire themselves. Eventually Becky began to conduct direct-mail campaigns to raise money for the organization. A key third person, Donna Wilcox, joined ACA to lead the organization in 1991. In 1997, ACA slowly added a few staff members. And in 1999, a woman called to get information about ACA and was so impressed with it that she gave a sizeable donation that allowed Alley Cat Allies to hire some more people and to free up Becky's time so she could do more advocacy work and less fundraising. She admits that none of this would have been possible if not for her husband, Ed Lytwak, who has supported her every day, including becoming the caregiver of their own cats and their feral cat colony.

The organization has undergone many changes over the years. In 2000, Louise left and Becky became the only founder at the helm. She and Donna have continued to fight the uphill battle for cats and have made major inroads. But it has not been easy. She went many years without an income, and she works almost all the time. When we talked, she was dealing with a situation in Nebraska where a police officer had trapped and shot a pet cat because it was in some trash. The owners were devastated. Despite animal cruelty laws and ordinances in that community, the officer received only a written reprimand and remains on the job. For some people, killing cats is perfectly acceptable. It's cultural, she explained. If there was one thing I learned from Becky it was that she was tenacious. I have no doubt that that town in Nebraska will be less likely to resort to such methods again.

PROGRESS

As Becky and I began to end our conversation, I asked, "Which areas of the country are the most progressive when it comes to feral cats?"

She answered without hesitation, "Arlington, Virginia; Austin, Texas; Chicago; Washington, DC; Fairfax, Virginia; Indianapolis, Indiana; Jacksonville, Florida; New York City; Philadelphia, Pennsylvania; Richmond, Virginia; and San Francisco, California, are the places that are most progressive right now."

"What makes them progressive?" I wanted to know

Again, her answer came quickly, "They don't mindlessly send animal control officers out to trap cats, they don't loan traps to the public, they don't frivolously impound cats, and they encourage TNR programs."

I was thrilled to learn that Chicago was one of the more progressive places, so I asked, "What more we could be doing here?"

"There is a tremendous need for low and no-cost spaying and neutering, free neutering before adoptions, nurseries for kittens so they can bottle feed and aren't euthanized, education of the public, and only euthanizing very sick and severely injured animals at shelters and animal control organizations. Currently, tax dollars pay for thousands and thousands of animals to be put down every year. Why not put that money to spaying and neutering these animals, finding them homes, and educating people?"

The last thing I asked her was, "Do you have any advice for colony caretakers?"

She paused for a moment and then replied, "People who take care of free-roaming cats are unsung heroes. Many of them have made great personal sacrifices. One caretaker lost his home because the people in his homeowner's association said that he and the cats had to go. Social change is never easy, but the ship is slowly turning. And we are part of a greater universe where we're all connected. Small actions can have big consequences. Those who take care of animals represent the very best part of our humanity."

My heart skipped a beat and sighed.

CHAPTER 27

Springtime and Summer in Chicago

SPRINGTIME FINALLY CAME TO CHICAGO, and life became a lot easier. No heating up food bowls, no heating discs to keep the food warm, and no more need to have a heated water bowl. But before spring arrived, we decided to invest in a cat condominium, complete with heated pads for the Rat Pack. The condo has two levels—one house above another one with a cat-sized porch on the front of each house. It is cedar with little shingles. Very cute. We decided that we wanted to give them a lovely place to live, given that they would be with us for many years. It was my husband's idea.

And we invested in a security system to monitor the cat's living area, as well as all the areas around our home. We didn't believe it was actually necessary, but it gave us peace of mind and allowed us to see what our furry friends were up to all of the time. I have reviewed hours of footage and learned quite a few things. One thing I didn't realize was that two other cats live in the area. And interestingly, my cats are friendly with them. One of them is a black-and-white-splotched cat, whom we named Jackson Pollock. The other, a large black cat, we named Nescafé. Both cats are large and, I think, male. Jackson came into our cats' area and then left with one of the girls. Later, I saw Duke playing with him. It was actually cute. I will be trapping both Jackson and Nescafé and getting them neutered soon.

Cat Condo

The other thing I've learned from reviewing the footage is how much time the cats spend with each other. They often play together, snuggle up to one another when they sleep, and seem to genuinely look after one another. I often see all three cats snuggled up together in their living area. They are clearly a small nuclear cat family.

As the days have become warmer and summer has arrived, the cats have spent more time outside playing in the yard. It has been fun to see them sneaking up on one another and tussling in the grass. They will hide under one of our hasta plants and then emerge chasing a bug or a butterfly. If you can imagine what a happy life is for a cat, then I think my cats' life would qualify for that designation. They get regular meals of wet and dry cat food and have a condominium to sleep in that's dry (and warm in the winter); they have each other to play with, neighbors around them who look out for them, and caretakers who have become very attached to them and watch them closely. They have all gained weight since they came to live with us, and their coats are sleek and shiny.

ALLIE, DUKE, AND ELOISE

Allie has lost some of her initial shyness. When she first came to our home, she would run away whenever I went into the cats' living area or got anywhere near her. But nowadays, she will slip by me and eat in front of me. And recently she let me take pictures of her after she woke up from a nap in the bushes. She also started to come up the front stairs one day as I came out with food, something she has never done before. Hopefully, over time, she will become less fearful.

Allie in the Bushes

Duke continues to be a playful young cat. She came to us when she was a kitten, and I soon learned that her weakness was cat toys. When the weather got warmer, I threw a small ball into the yard, and Duke played for a long time with it, throwing it around and chasing it. We still occasionally refer to her as "he" or "him" because we thought she was a boy. She can often be found snuggling up with Allie and Eloise. Recently she let me pet her while she was eating.

Eloise remains her sweet self and will always be found waiting for me at the bottom or the top of the steps at mealtime. And if she's playing in the yard, she will often start meowing and come to me if she sees me. She has become less fearful over time and loves to be petted. She is incredibly sweet with me but terribly ferocious when it comes to rats. I have seen her more than a few times with a rat that she has caught.

As we reflect back on the time that we have had these creatures in our world, both my husband and I never realized how effective they would be at getting rid of our rat problem, how much we would care for them, and the impact they would have on our lives. Our journey continues, and I look forward to the future.

Fun in the Backyard

Allie and Duke

References

Alley Cat Allies. 2014a. "Trap-Neuter-Return Effectively Stabilizes and Reduces Feral Cat Populations." http://www.alleycat.org/tnrworks. Accessed April 23, 2014.

———. 2014b. "The Vacuum Effect: Why Catch and Kill Doesn't Work." http://www.alleycat.org/Page.aspx?pid=926. Accessed April 23, 2014.

ASPCA. 2014. "Position Statement on Feral Cat Management. http://www.aspca.org/about-us/aspca-policy-and-position-statements/position-statement-on-feral-cat-management. Accessed May 3, 2014.

Baker, P. J., S. E. Molony, E. Stone, I. C. Cuthill, and S. Harris. 2008. "Cats about Town: Is Predation by Free-Ranging Pet cats *Felis catus* Likely to Affect Urban Bird Populations?" *Ibis* 150: Supplement 1, 86–99. http://www.ingentaconnect.com/content/bsc/ibi/2008/00000150/A00101s1/art00008.

Beall, A. E. 2010. *Strategic Market Research*. Bloomington: iUniverse.

Blanton, J.D., D. Palmer, J. Dyer, and C. E. Rupprecht. 2011, "Rabies Surveillance in the United States during 2010." *Journal of American Veterinary Medical Association* 239 (6): 773–83.

Centers for Disease Control and Prevention (CDC). 2014a. "Human Rabies." http://www.cdc.gov/rabies/location/usa/surveillance/human_rabies.html. Accessed April 21, 2014.

———. 2014b. "Diseases from Cats." http://www.cdc.gov/healthypets/animals/cats.htm. Accessed April 21, 2014.

Crooks, K. R. and M. E. Soulé. 1999. "Mesopredator Release and Avifaunal Extinctions in a Fragmented System." *Nature* 400: 563–66.

Doyle, B. 2013. "Feral Cats Act Draws a Crowd." *Chicago Tribune*, March 19, 2013. http://articles.chicagotribune.com/2013-03-19/news/ct-met-feral-cat-hearing-20130320_1_cat-advocates-yvette-pina-neuter-and-release. Accessed April 30, 2014.

The Global Invasive Species Database. 2010. "Felis catus (mammal)." http://www.issg.org/database/species/ecology.asp?si=24&fr=1&sts=&lang=EN. Accessed May 3, 2014.

Hughes, K. L. and M. R. Slater. 2002. "Implementation of a Feral Cat Management Program on a University Campus." *Journal of Applied Animal Welfare Science* 5 (1): 15–28.

Ji, W., S. D. Sarre, N. Aitken, R. K. S. Hankin, and M. N. Clout. 2001 "Sex-Biased Dispersal and a Density-Independent Mating System in the Australian Brushtail Possum, as Revealed by Minisatelite DNA Profiling." *Molecular Ecology* 10 (2001): 1527–37.

Jones, A. and C. Downs. 2011 "Managing Feral Cats on a University's Campuses: How Many Are There and Is Sterilization Having an Effect?" *Journal of Applied Animal Welfare Science* 14 (4): 304–20.

Kays, R.W. and A. A. DeWan. 2004. "Ecological Impact of Inside/Outside House Cats around a Suburban Nature Preserve." *Animal Conservation* 7: 273–83.

Killian, G., K. Fagerstone, T. Kreeger, L. Miller, and J. Rhyan. 2007. "Management Strategies for Addressing Wildlife Disease Transmission: The Case for Fertility Control." *U.S.D.A National Wildlife Research Center.* http://www.aphis.usda.gov/wildlife_damage/nwrc/publications/07pubs/fagerstone071.pdf. Accessed April 23, 2014.

LA Times. 2009. "Advocates Report Success with Trap, Neuter, Return Approach to Stray Cats." September, 29, 2014. http://latimesblogs. latimes.com/unleashed/2009/09/advocates-report-success-with-trap-neuter-return-approach-to-stray-cats.html. Accessed April 23, 2014.

Levy, J. K., D. W. Gale, and L. A. Gale. 2003. "Evaluation of the Effect of a Long-Term Trap-Neuter-Return and Adoption Program on a Free-Roaming Cat Population." *Journal of the American Veterinary Medical Association* 222: 42–46.

Loss, S. R., T. Will, and P. P. Marra. 2013. "The Impact of Free-Ranging Domestic Cats on Wildlife of the United States." *Nature Communications*. 4: 1396.

Loyd, K. T., S. M. Hernandez, J. P. Carroll, K. J. Abernathy, and G. J. Marshall. 2013. "Quantifying Free-Roaming Domestic Cat Predation Using Animal-Borne Video Cameras." *Biological Conservation* 160: 183–89.

Mitchell, J. C. and R. A. Beck. 1992. "Free-Ranging Domestic Cat Predation on Native Vertebrates in Rural and Urban Virginia." *Virginia Journal of Science* 43: 197–207.

Moller, A. P. and J. Erritzoe. 2000. "Predation against Birds with Low Immunocompetence." *Oecolgia* 122 (4): 500–504.

Morris, D. 2011. *Catwatching*. New York: Random House.

Morrissey, C. 2013. "Project Bay Cat Helps San Francisco Bay's Rock-Dwelling Kitties." *Catster*. http://www.catster.com/lifestyle/project-bay-cat-san-francisco.

Natoli, E., L. Maragliano, G. Cariola, A. Faini, R. Bonanni, S. Cafazzo, and C. Fantino. 2006. "Management of Feral Domestic Cats in the Urban Environment of Rome (Italy)." *Preventative Veterinary Medicine* 77: 180–85.

Rich, T. D., C. J. Beardmore, H. Berlanga, P. J. Blancher, M. S. W. Bradstreet, G. S. Butcher, D. W. Demarest, E. H. Dunn, W. C. Hunter, E. E. Iñigo-Elias, J. A. Kennedy, A. M. Martell, A. O. Panjabi, D. N. Pashley, K. V. Rosenberg, C. M. Rustay, J. S. Wendt, and T. C. Will. 2004. "Partners in Flight North American Landbird Conservation Plan." Cornell Lab of Ornithology. Ithaca, NY. www.partnersinflight. org/cont_plan/.

Partners in Flight Science Committee. 2013. PIF Population Estimates Database, version 2.0 (2013). http://rmbo.org/pifpopestimates. Accessed on April 14, 2014.

Royal Society for the Protection of Birds (RSPB). 2014. "Are Cats Causing Bird Declines?" http://www.rspb.org.uk/advice/gardening/ unwantedvisitors/cats/birddeclines.aspx. Accessed May 3, 2014.

Stoskopf, M. and F. Nutter, F. 2004. "Analyzing Approaches to Feral Cat Management: One Size Does Not Fit All." *Journal of American Veterinary Medical Association* 225 (9): 1361–64.

Wolf, P. J. 2013. "The Greater Threat Is Junk Science: An Open Letter to the AVMA." http://www.voxfelina.com/2013/05/the-greater-threat-is-junk-science-an-open-letter-to-the-avma. Accessed April 30, 2014.

Appendix A–
Cat Survey

Beall Research, Inc.
333 N. Michigan Ave, Suite 415
Chicago IL 60601
(312) 384-1214

OBJECTIVES

- » Estimate the number of owned cats in the United States

- » Estimate the number of free-roaming (stray/feral) cats in the United States

- » Identify current attitudes toward free-roaming cats in the United States

- » Determine current reactions to TNR programs

- » Ascertain which messaging is most effective for persuading about TNR

- » Determine which messaging is most effective for persuading pet owners to spay/neuter cats

QUALIFICATIONS

- » Eighteen to eighty years old

- » Must be a US resident

QUOTAS

Males	750
Females	750
TOTAL	**1,500**

Quota for cat owners = 250 (contained within 1,500)

Geographic quotas to represent the US population

PROGRAMMING LANGUAGE IS IN CAPS AND WAS
NOT SHOWN TO RESPONDENTS.

SCREENER

S.1   What is your gender? (*Select one.*)

Males		
Females		
TOTAL		

S.2   What year were you born? (*Enter year.*)

Year born		

DISPLAY: Please answer *both* this question about Hispanic origin and the following question about race. For this study, Hispanic origin is not a race.

S.3   Are you of Hispanic, Latino, or Spanish origin? (*Select one.*)

Yes		
No		

S.4   Which of the following best describes your race? (*Select all that apply.*)

White or Caucasian		
African American or Black		
Asian		
Native American or Alaskan Native		
Native Hawaiian or other Pacific Islander		
Some other ethnicity (*please specify*)		

S.5   Which of the following categories best represents your annual *household* income before taxes in 2013? (*Select one.*)

Less than $10,000		
$10,000–$14,999		
$15,000–$24,999		
$25,000–$34,999		

$35,000–$49,999		
$50,000–$74,999		
$75,000–$99,999		
$100,000–$149,999		
$150,000–$199,999		
$200,000 or more		
Prefer not to answer		TERMINATE

S.6　In which state do you live? (*Select one.*)

State list shown		

S.7　Do you currently have any of the following pets? (*Select all that apply.*)

Bird		
Cat		
Dog		
Gerbil or hamster		
None of the above		

SEE QUOTA OF 250 FOR CAT OWNERS. IF CAT NOT SELECTED, SKIP TO S.9

S.8　How many of the cats in your household live indoors 100 percent of the time? *Do not include any cats that live outdoors 100 percent of the time. We will ask about them in the next question. (Enter number for each row.)*

Number cats in your household who *live inside* 100 percent of the time		OWNED INDOOR
Number of cats in your household who *live indoors and go outside*		OWNED INDOOR-OUTSIDE
TOTAL INDOOR CATS		SUM TERMINATE IF >50

134

S.9 How many cats *live outdoors* on your property? Please include stray and feral cats even if you see very infrequently. (*Enter number for each row.*) If there are none, please enter "0."

For the purposes of this survey, *feral cats* are cats that are born in the wild. They are different from *stray cats*, which are pet cats that have been lost or abandoned and were not born in the wild. The two types of cats look the same.

Number of *stray or feral cats* on your property *whom you **do not feed***		NOT FED STRAY/FERAL
Number of *stray or feral cats* on your property *whom you **feed regularly***		FED STRAY/ FERAL CATS
Number of cats in your household who live outside 100 percent of the time *whom you feed* and ***who are not stray or feral cats***		OWNED OUTSIDE
TOTAL OUTDOOR CATS		SUM TERMINATE IF > 150

IF S.7 "CAT" SELECTED, BUT HAVE TOTAL OF 0 IN S.8 AND S.9, TERMINATE.
IF FED STRAY/FERAL CATS > 0, ASK S.10.

S.10 Do you currently have a feral cat colony that you regularly feed? A feral cat colony is a group of feral cats that lives in a single place for a sustained period of time. (*Select one.*)

Yes		CLASSIFY AS FERAL COLONY
No		SKIP TO A.1

S.11 How many cats are in your feral cat colony? (*Enter number.*)

Number of cats in feral cat colony		

MAIN QUESTIONNAIRE

General Attitudes toward Stray Cats

A.1 Which of the following best describes your feelings about *stray cats*? (*Select all that apply.*)

I don't mind them		
I feel sorry for them		
I wish I could help them		
I consider them to be pests		
I consider them to be dangerous		
I try to help them when I can		
I am afraid of them		
I don't have any feelings about stray cats		
I hate stray cats		
I hate all cats		
Other (*please specify*)		

IF "HATE STRAY CATS" OR "HATE ALL CATS" SELECTED
IN A.1, THEN CONTINUE; ELSE SKIP TO A.3.

A.2 What are the major reasons that you hate cats? (*Select all that apply.*)

I have been bitten by cats in the past		
I have been scratched by cats in the past		
Cats are aloof and too independent		
Cats carry diseases		
My family has always hated cats		
Cats shed hair everywhere		
Cats bother my dogs		
Cats don't like me		
Cats are a nuisance		

I am fearful of cats		
Cats are snobby		
Other (*please specify*)		

A.3   If you saw a stray cat in your community and could only choose between two courses of action—leaving the cat where it is outside or having the cat caught and then put down—which would you consider to be the more humane option for the cat? (*Select one.*)

Leave the cat where it is		
Have the cat put down		
Don't know		
Other (*please specify*)		

A.4   If you knew that the stray cat you saw would die in two years because it would be hit by a car, which would you consider the most humane option today? (*Select one.*)

Leave the cat where it is and let it live two years before dying		
Have the cat put down		
Don't know		
Other (*please specify*)		

Attitudes toward TNR

Some of the cats you see outside are *feral cats*. Feral cats are cats that are born in the wild. They are different from *stray cats*, which are pet cats that have been lost or abandoned and were not born in the wild. The two types of cats do not look different.

There is a simple program to help feral cats. It's called the *trap-neuter-return* (TNR) program. With TNR programs, feral cats are humanely trapped and then spayed or neutered so they can't have kittens. After they have recovered from surgery, they are relocated or returned to their original location.

This program stabilizes and *reduces feral cat populations* and improves the cats' lives. The behaviors associated with mating, such as yowling, spraying, and fighting stop after cats are spayed or neutered.

B.0   Before this survey, had you ever heard of the trap-neuter-return (TNR) program before? (*Select one.*)

I had not heard of this program		
I had heard of it but *didn't know much about it*		
I have heard of it and *knew something about it*		
I have heard of it and am *very familiar with it*		

B.1   What is your attitude toward Trap-Neuter-Return (TNR) programs? Please answer using a 10-point scale where 1 means "Extremely negative" and 10 means "Extremely positive."

Attitude toward TNR		

B.2   What are the reasons for your rating? (*Enter response below.*)

B.3   Below is some information about *trap-neuter-return (TNR) programs.* How important is the following information to you? Please answer using a 10-point scale where 1 means "Not at all important" and 10 means "Extremely important." (*Enter ratings.*)
RANDOMIZE PRESENTATION

TNR programs have been shown to stabilize and reduce the feral-cat populations		

Cats who are part of TNR programs have been successfully used to get rid of rats and mice		
Cats in TNR programs have *not* been shown to significantly reduce bird populations		
Cats in TNR programs are shown to live as long as cats who are indoors		
Cats in TNR programs are monitored for diseases and have not been shown to be a health hazard		
Cats in TNR programs are less likely to fight (because they have been spayed or neutered) and they are less likely to be injured by other cats		
Cats in TNR programs belong in a colony where they are regularly fed by a colony caretaker and therefore do not have to hunt for their food		
Cats in TNR programs are fed by a caretaker and are similar in size and weight to indoor cats		
Cats in TNR programs live in urban, suburban, and rural areas and have been effective at reducing the number of rats in those areas		
Cats in TNR programs are regularly vaccinated and are not at risk to transmit rabies or other feline diseases to other cats		

Local humane societies monitor feral cat colonies and ensure they are being properly cared for		
Local humane societies are generally the ones who trap, neuter, and return/relocate the cats		
Please select a "4" for quality control purposes		

IF MORE THAN 1 ITEM RATED 8, 9, OR 10 IN B.3 THEN ASK B.4 DISPLAYING THOSE ITEMS. IF ONLY ONE ITEM RATED 8, 9, OR 10, THEN BACKFILL TO B.4 AND SKIP TO B.5. IF NO ITEM RATED 8, 9, OR 10, SELECT TOP-RATED ITEMS AND SHOW IN B.4.

IF ONLY ONE ITEM RATED HIGHEST, BUT LESS THE 8, 9, OR 10, WILL BACKFILL AND SKIP B.4. IF TWO OR MORE ITEMS EQUALLY RATED HIGHEST (LESS THE 8, 9, OR 10) ASK B.4.

B.4   Of the information presented, which one is most important to you? (*Select one.*)

DISPLAY ITEMS FROM B.3		

B.5   Given that [DISPLAY ITEM FROM B.4], does this information make you feel much more positively or much more negatively about TNR programs? Please answer using a 10-point scale where 1 means "Much more negatively" and 10 means "Much more positively." (*Enter rating.*)

Impact on feelings about TNR programs		

B.6   If there were a free trap-neuter-return program in your area, how likely would you be *to support such a program? By support, we do not mean financial support.* Please answer using a 10-point scale where 1 means "Extremely unlikely to support" and 10 means "Extremely likely to support." (*Enter rating.*)

Likelihood to support TNR program		

DO NOT ASK B.7 OF COLONY CARETAKERS (S.10 = YES).

B.7   If there were a trap-neuter-return program in your area, how *likely would you be to become a colony caretaker* if you knew it involved feeding feral cats twice a day and monitoring their health? Please answer using a 10-point scale where 1 means "'Extremely unlikely" and 10 means "Extremely likely.' (*Enter rating.*)

Likelihood to become a colony caretaker		

B.8   Which of the following statements best represents your attitudes about putting down cats in pet shelters? (*Select one.*)

I believe that shelters should put down cats when there are too many of them		
I believe that shelters should only put down cats when they are either too ill or too aggressive to be adopted		
Other (*please specify*)		

Attitudes toward Spaying/Neutering Cats

ASK CAT OWNERS (S.8 > 0)

C.1   How many of your [INSERT NUMBER FROM S.8] cats who live indoors are neutered/spayed—meaning they have been "fixed" and cannot have kittens. (*Enter number.*)

Number		CALCULATE PERCENTAGE OF CATS WHO ARE NEUTERED/SPAYED C.1/S.8*100

C.2   How important is it to spay/neuter cats so they cannot reproduce and have kittens? Please answer using a 10-point scale where 1 means "Not at all important" and 10 means "Extremely Important." (*Enter rating.*)

Number		

C.3   What are the reasons for your rating? (*Enter response below.*)

C.4   Below is some information about *spaying/neutering*. How important is the following information to you? Please answer using a 10-point scale where 1 means "Not at all important" and 10 means "Extremely important." (*Enter ratings.*) RANDOMIZE PRESENTATION.

Cats who are not spayed/ neutered are more likely to fight with other cats		
Cats who are not spayed/ neutered are more likely to spray their urine inside and outside		
Cats who are not spayed/neutered are more likely to howl at night		
There is already an overpopulation of cats in the United States, and over 1.5 million cats are put down every year		
There are very few no-kill shelters in the United States, and the animal shelters put down 70 percent of cats and kittens brought to them each year		

The majority of kittens and cats taken to shelters are never adopted		
Cats who have been spayed/ neutered live longer than those who have not		
There are veterinarians who offer low cost or no-cost spays/neutering		
There are programs that offer free transportation for spaying/neutering		
The vast majority of kittens who are under five weeks of age are generally put down at shelters because they are not weaned and require bottle feeding every few hours		
Kittens begin reproducing at about four to six months of age		
Indoor cats will not display many annoying mating behaviors (for example, howling, spraying, pleading to go out) if they are spayed/neutered		
Please select a "4" for quality control purposes		

IF MORE THAN 1 ITEM RATED 8, 9, OR 10 IN C.4, THEN ASK C.5, DISPLAYING THOSE ITEMS. IF ONLY ONE ITEM RATED 8, 9, OR 10, THEN BACKFILL TO C.5 AND SKIP TO C.6. IF NO ITEM RATED 8, 9, OR 10, SELECT TOP-RATED ITEMS AND SHOW IN C.5

C.5   Of the information presented, which one is most important to you? (*Select one.*)

DISPLAY ITEMS FROM C.4		

C.6 Given that [DISPLAY ITEM FROM C.5], does this information make you feel much more positively or much more negatively about spaying/neutering? Please answer using a 10-point scale where 1 means "Much more negatively" and 10 means "Much more positively." (*Enter rating.*)

Impact on feelings about spaying/neutering		

IF OWN CATS AND SPAYS/NEUTERS NOT 100 PERCENT, ASK C.7

C.7 Given this information, how likely are you to spay/neuter your cats that are not currently spayed/neutered? Please answer using a 10-point scale where 1 means "Extremely unlikely" and 10 means "Extremely likely." (*Enter rating.*)

Likelihood to spay/neuter		

Demographics/Catographics

IF OWNED INDOORS OR OWNED INDOORS-OUTSIDE > 0, ASK Z.2–Z.5.

Z.1 DELETED

Z.2 Of the [INSERT TOTAL NUMBER OF CATS FROM S.8] cats who live inside your home, how old are they? Enter the number of cats for each age below. (*Enter number for cats for each age group.*)

	Number of cats who live in your home
Less than 1 year	
1–2 years	
3–5 years	
6–10 years	
11–15 years	
16–20 years	
21–25 years	
26 years or older	

Z.3 Of the [INSERT TOTAL NUMBER OF CATS FROM S.8] cats who live inside your home, where did you get each one? Enter the number of cats for each place below. *(Enter number for cats for each age group.)*

	Number of cats who live in your home who came from each place
From a pet store	
From a cattery or breeder	
From a pet shelter	
From the outside—it was a stray	
From a friend or family member	
Other *(please specify)*	

Z.4 How long have you had cats as pets? *(Select one.)*

Less than 1 year		
1–5 years		
6–10 years		
11–20 years		
21–30 years		
31–40 years		
41–50 years		
51+ years		

Z.5 How many cats have you had in your lifetime as pets? *(Enter number.)*

Number of pet cats		

ASK IF ANY OWNED INDOOR-OUTSIDE > 0

Z.6 Do your cats that live indoors but go outdoors do any of the following? *(Select all that apply.)*

Eat grass		
Eat flowers		

Eat other plants		
Kill rats		
Kill mice		
Kill birds		
Kill rabbits		
Kill other animals (*please specify*)		
None of the above		
Don't know		

IF DID NOT SELECT RATS IN Z.6, THEN BACKFILL
ZERO AND SKIP TO Z.8; ELSE CONTINUE.

Z.7 About how may rats *in total* are all your cats killing in an average year? Please *provide a total number for all the cats who live indoors* to the best of your knowledge. (*Enter number.*)

Don't know		

IF DID NOT SELECT BIRDS IN Z.6, THEN BACKFILL
ZERO AND SKIP TO Z.9; ELSE CONTINUE.

Z.8 About how may birds *in total* are all your cats killing in an average year? Please *provide a total number for all your cats who live indoors* to the best of your knowledge. (*Enter number.*)

Don't know		

ASK Z.9–Z.11 IF OWNED OUTSIDE OR FED STRAY/
FERAL OR UNFED STRAY FERAL > 0.

The next section is about cats that live outdoors all the time.

Z.9 Do the cats around your home that live outdoors do any of the following (*Select all that apply.*)

Eat grass		
Eat flowers		

Eat other plants		
Kill rats		
Kill mice		
Kill birds		
Kill rabbits		
Kill other animals (*please specify*)		
None of the above		
Don't know		

IF DID NOT SELECT RATS IN Z.9, THEN BACKFILL ZERO AND SKIP TO Z.11; ELSE CONTINUE.

Z.10 About how many rats *in total* are all the cats killing in an average year? Please provide a total number for all the cats around your home to the best of your knowledge—do not include cats who live indoors. (*Enter number.*)

Don't know		

IF DID NOT SELECT BIRDS IN Z.9, THEN BACKFILL ZERO AND SKIP TO Z.12; ELSE CONTINUE.

Z.11 About how may birds *in total* are all your cats killing in an average year? Please provide a total number for all the cats around your home to the best of your knowledge—do not include cats who live indoors. (*Enter number.*)

Don't know		

Z.12 How many people under 18 are living in your home? (*Select one.*)

None		
1		
2		
3		
4		
5 or more		

Z.13 Which of the following best describes the area where you live (primary residence)? *(Select one.)*

Urban/Large city		
Suburban/Small city		
Rural/Small town		

Z.14 How many of the following pets do have? *(Enter number. If you do not own any, please enter 0.)*

Z.15 Is there anything else you would like to share about cats? If so, please feel free to enter it below. *(Enter response.)*

DISPLAY: *Thank you for participating in our study.*

Appendix B–
Calculation Methods

Number of Households in the United States	121,122,161	
Number of households with indoor cats that go outdoors and kill birds	4.67%	5,652,367
Average number of birds killed by indoor cats that go outdoors for each household in one year	1.2	
Total number of birds killed by indoor cats that can go outdoors in one year	**6,782,841**	
Number of households with outdoor cats (including stray/feral) who kill birds	8.93%	10,820,246
Average number of birds killed by all outdoor cats for each household in one year	1.37	
Total number or birds killed by all outdoor cats in one year	**14,823,737**	
Total birds killed in one year by cats	**21,606,578**	

Calculation for number of birds killed by indoor cats that go outdoors

121,122,161 * Number of household with indoor cats that go outdoors and kill birds (4.67%) = 5,652,367 households

5,652,367 * Number of birds killed by indoor cats that go outdoors in one year (1.2) = 6,782,841

Calculation for number of birds killed by outdoor cats

121,122,161 * Number of household with outdoor cats (including stray/feral) who kill birds (8.93%) = 10,820,246 households

10,820,246 * Number of birds killed by indoor cats that go outdoors in one year (1.37) = 14,823,737

Total number of birds killed = number of birds killed by indoor cats (6,782,841) + number of birds killed by outdoor cats (14,823,737) = 21,606,578

CPSIA information can be obtained
at www.ICGtesting.com
Printed in the USA
LVOW12s1730141016

508827LV00001B/159/P